AFTER

EVEREST

An Autobiography
by

TENZING NORGAY

Conqueror of Chomolungma

London

This edition first published by Gibson Square

www.gibsonsquare.com

The moral right of Tenzing Norgay to be identified as the author of this work has been asserted in accordance with the Copyright, Designs and Patents Act 1988.

Many people have helped, especially with information, in making this story, notably June Kirkwood, Lute Jerstad, Stan Armington, Sally Westmacott, Norman Hardie, Achille Compagnoni, Raymond Lambert, Albert Eggler, Ernst Feuz, Charles Wylie, and Tenzing's unnamed helpers who read my many letters to him and wrote for him the replies to my innumerable questions. The library of the Alpine Club has been invaluable for checking information; so has the Swiss Foundation for Alpine Research. Most of the photographs were supplied by Tenzing himself, but others were supplied by Dolf Reist of Interlaken, the Swiss Foundation, Das Studios of Darjeeling; acknowledgements are given elsewhere. MEB

CONTENTS

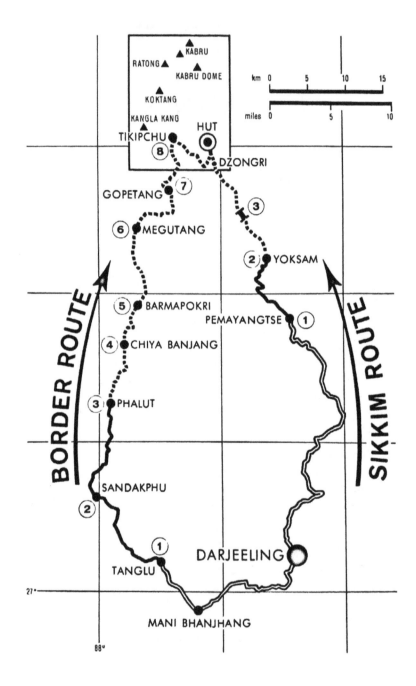

1: NEVER THE SAME AGAIN

Twenty years and more have passed since the summit of Mount Everest was first reached by man and I stood with Edmund Hillary at the highest point on earth late in the morning of 29 May 1953. Twenty years is a long time in a man's life, and a long time too in a quick-changing world. Many years and a lot of effort had brought me a little unexpectedly to that high and lonely place in the thin air, under an incredibly blue sky, with a whole world of mountains spread out around and below us. I was nearly forty years of age. It was my seventh expedition to the mountain and the fulfilment of a dream. It was also the fulfilment of the efforts of a whole generation and more of climbing men, who in their own ways had had the same dream as mine, so if the achievement created a sensation it is not surprising. It was celebrated throughout the world, though differently with each people.

It was in fact a most important moment. The news of our success was intentionally delayed and was only broadcast in Britain some days later, on Coronation Day, 2 June. But we had a long march back and everyone knew about the ascent of Everest long before we returned to civilisation. Then in Nepal and in India people went crazy. Politically-minded men rushed in to gain some benefit from my own part in the climb, invented stories about it and twisted the truth, proclaiming me the hero of Nepal, of India, or of the East, and so on, simply because I had been lucky enough and persistent enough to reach the top of the world and the headlines of the newspapers too.

This was a difficult time for everybody in the expedition. I could not help being pleased at this personal reception; anyone would be. But the attempt to split me from Edmund Hillary and the rest of the expedition and to create trouble amongst us was really frightening and it has left a dark mark on my memory of our victory. Also the frenzy of the crowds was almost terrifying, even before we got to Kathmandu, though worse afterwards, and so were the mobs of excited pressmen who never left us for a moment.

Now it seems hard to believe the excitement; it is such a very long time ago, and so much has happened since then that the significance of the event no longer seems as great, no longer seems real, even to me, but especially to a generation that has been born or has grown up in the interval. They cannot remember it anyway.

Even then, in 1953, I had the feeling that nothing would ever be the same again—for me, for the Sherpas, for Solu Khumbu, for mountaineering as a sport. And nothing was. It was not that by climbing Everest nothing was left for the mountaineers to do. Not at all. Rather the reverse. Now there was everything to do; nothing was beyond man's ambition and there was plenty of that everywhere.

The sport grew as never before, especially in the Himalaya because they offered the most ambitious and the most varied climbing of any range in the world. And in growing it gave me a career I would not have thought about a few years earlier. The great Himalayan and Karakorum summits that had not so far been climbed—they were many—began to fall one after the other to expeditions from many lands: Kangchenjunga, Makalu, Pumori, K2, Dhaulagiri, Cho Oyu, Nuptse, Lhotse, Manaslu, Broad Peak…. The list of those that were climbed in the next few years is very long indeed, and of course there were casualties, many casualties, among the Sherpas too. In a year or two few of the really famous main summits remained unclimbed, though there are to this day numbers of mountains still unclimbed—secondary summits, of course, but still very big ones. Anyway, after Everest nothing seemed impossible.

This is what the event meant for mountaineering in the Himalaya: a sort of obstacle -physical, mental—had disappeared and the flood of expeditions came in. Of course, it caused plenty of practical problems in the area. For one thing, the mountains now had to be shared out among the eager rival expeditions; permission to climb the peaks had to be applied for very early and the popular ones were soon booked up for a year or two in advance. The authorities simply did not want an unregulated scramble for the peaks. Supplies of everything from food to porters were not unlimited, and as a result of the invasion there were times of quite serious shortages. At one point all expeditions in Nepal were stopped completely by the Government for a time.

For me personally the change was rather different, and that is the main subject of this book; my life took on a new direction. As for the Sherpa people who live on the road to Everest—and had lived there undisturbed for centuries— also for the rest of Nepal, from now on fully open to the world, the changes were very serious and this is the other subject of my book.

Since that great moment when Edmund Hillary and I shook hands on a high patch of snow, looked down on the huge panorama of peaks and glaciers and valleys and clouds, and remembered for a moment or two—we were only on the summit for about fifteen minutes – those who had tried before us and failed, then thanked God for our own success and prayed for a safe descent, and scratched in the snow to bury little things like a pencil and a bag of sweets and a cat made of black cloth—since that moment a new generation of men and women have been born both in Solu Khumbu and in the world outside that now wonders what the fuss was about. You would have to be nearly thirty years old today actually to remember it and you would have to be really middle-aged to have taken part in the celebrations and listened to the lectures given by the climbers when they got home. I have been strongly aware of this in recent times when talking about Everest to groups of people in distant places and realising the age of those who really understood what I was talking about. I am not saying that the young do not enjoy the story. They do, just as they enjoy all good adventure stories, on the mountains or on the sea or anywhere else.

It is like this: for the final ascent of Everest there was a long build-up for the climbers themselves and for those who followed the adventure. For me too. For everyone therefore the ascent in 1953 was a great climax. For many, many years, ever since Everest was recognised as the earth's highest mountain, men had tried to conquer it. It was almost a permanent challenge. Mostly they tried by the northern route through Tibet, and all had failed, though there were some tremendous achievements, especially when you take into account the real lack of knowledge of very great heights and what was needed to survive them, also the primitiveness of much of the equipment and clothing and supplies, and finally the mental attitudes which held people in check. For me it was very interesting, for instance, to compare what I saw of the expeditions from the north before the war with those from the south, two with the Swiss in 1952 and one with the British in 1953. Of course, in experience and information there was no comparison and the equipment bore no resemblance to older times. You have only to look at the photographs to see the difference, especially the clothing, the boots—and even hats! Yet the will to succeed was the same and very great skill and courage. How else could Mallory and Irvine have got as high as they did with all those disadvantages—some say that they actually got to the top and fell on the descent? Others, too, like Smythe, Norton, Somerville, Odell, who got very close to succeeding.

So our excitement in the end is very understandable, I think, the sense of accomplishment at having done so much at last, climbing on the backs, one might say, of all those who had gone before, Sherpas as well as Europeans; for quite a few of my own people had died on those expeditions and among those who did not die were some who got very high on the mountain.

I can only give a very personal story of what has happened since 1953. In the book which James Ramsay Ullman wrote down for me after a long time spent in giving him the spoken story, I told of my beginnings, what set me on the road to Everest and the many adventures I had until then. There would be no point in repeating them here; in *Tiger of the Snows* the details are all to be found. Yet for the benefit of readers who do not remember those days and have not read my first book, I must repeat very briefly those facts which they need to know if the story of what happened afterwards is to be understood.

My name is Tenzing Norgay and I am a Sherpa; that is to say, I am of Tibetan race, for it was from Tibet that our people came, as I shall explain. I was born in Thami, a village close to all the great mountains of the Everest region and on the way from Namche Bazar to the Nangpa-La, a high pass into Tibet. I was the eleventh of thirteen children and we were very poor until after I was born, when our herd of yaks began to grow until eventually it numbered some three or four hundred beasts. From then on we were modestly prosperous.

But my name was not always Tenzing Norgay. My mother's name was Kinzom and my father's was Ghang-La Mingma. Amongst our people a child does not usually take a family name. In fact, I was first called Namgyal Wangdi, and my present name was given me on the insistence of a lama who had found from the holy books that I was the reincarnation of a rich man of Solu Khumbu who had recently died. Tenzing Norgay was not that rich man's name, but the lama thought that a name that meant 'wealthy-fortunate follower of religion' would be best for one for whom he predicted great things.

My early days were spent looking after the yaks in the high pastures where I would go with them to the height of about 18,000 feet. There the grass ended and the rocks and glaciers began. And there it was that the dream—or ambition, call it what you like—took shape that drove me eventually through many adventures to the top of Everest, and afterwards to many parts of the civilised world. For around me in the pastures of the Himalaya stood the great mountains, Makalu, Lhotse, Cho Oyu, Nuptse, Pumori, Ama Dablam, and yes, Everest itself. Not all of them at any one time necessarily visible, but they were there in the foreground of my life. Even as a boy I had heard tales of the men who had tried to climb Everest from the other side. Other, older Sherpas had been with them and had brought the story back. Already I wanted to see it all for myself. So, when I was eighteen years old, that is in 1932, I left home and went to Darjeeling—where many Sherpas have always gone to seek a living—with the main intention of trying to join an expedition. Since then I have lived in Darjeeling continuously— for one thing it has been necessary for my work as a mountaineer—but it is one of the reasons for a certain amount of hostility to me in my native country of Nepal, not whilst I was unknown but only since I acquired fame on Everest. I did not succeed, however, in joining the 1933 expedition and it went off without me. Meanwhile I found other work to do and I married.

My first expedition to Everest was in 1935, the year my son Nima Dorje was born; it was the fifth British expedition to the mountain. On that attempt I was one of those who carried loads to North Col at over 22,000 feet; not bad for a beginner! But unlike some of the Sherpas, it was not for the wages alone—they were small enough anyway—that I climbed, but from some other urge, to go high and still higher on that mountain.

There was another expedition to Everest the following year, when again I reached North Col; but the weather was fearful and the snow impossibly soft and deep, so we had to give up. And another expedition, also unsuccessful, in 1938, my third, when I went as high as 27,200 feet—less than 2,000 feet from the top—and that was when I acquired my 'Tiger' medal. In between times there were expeditions elsewhere—Nanda Devi, Bandar Punch, Tirich Mir, Nanga Parbat, for instance. Later, after the war, there were journeys into the mountains with Swiss climbers, and of course that wonderful year-long journey into Tibet with Professor Tucci. But I got my fourth chance to climb Everest when I accompanied that lone climber, Earl Denman, in 1947—again from the north—and had to turn back below the col. That had been an extraordinary adventure, even though I had not gone as high as before; for we approached the mountain on foot all the way from Darjeeling, through Sikkim and Tibet, which we were forbidden to enter. I may say that the weather conditions on the mountain were appalling. My account of Everest seems so much concerned with bad weather and especially the raging gales; but this is typical of the mountain, and indeed of the whole region, as other peoples' experience proves.

Then came the Swiss in 1952—after probing expeditions through Nepal by others the previous year—and they asked for me as sirdar of their expedition. This was the one on which Raymond Lambert from Geneva and I got so near to the top, within 800 feet of it, and had been forced back again!—by the terrible wind. In the autumn of the same year we tried again—my sixth Everest expedition—and that was a failure too. Last in the series, so far as I was concerned, for my life changed abruptly afterwards, came the British expedition under Colonel John Hunt, later knighted and now Lord Hunt; this was the expedition on which, with Edmund Hillary, afterwards knighted too, I reached the summit not only of the highest mountain on earth but also of my ambitions.

Now for a word about the name 'Sherpa', which will often be used in this book and many people seem to think means simply 'mountain porter'—or at best 'mountain guide'—in the Himalaya. It means nothing of the kind, though so many Sherpas have taken up the work that the man and the job have come to mean the same thing. In reality, Sherpa is the name of a mountain tribe—to which I belong – who came over the high passes from Tibet a long time ago and settled in the high valleys and uplands of the eastern Himalaya, especially in what is known as the Solu Khumbu, on the road to Everest. Solu Khumbu is roughly the valley of the Dudh Kosi ('Milky River'); the lower part of the valley is known as Solu and the higher part as Khumbu. Most of the mountaineering Sherpas come from the higher part, Khumbu. Our language is also called Sherpa, a kind of Tibetan, and our religion, Buddhist, is of the Tibetan kind. Our traditions and customs are Tibetan too. There is still very close contact between the Sherpas of Nepal and their cousins in Tibet, and the communist occupation of Tibet has made only a small difference. The traffic over the passes is continuous even today.

Throughout the years many young Sherpas have gone south to Darjeeling, mostly in search of work, either in the tea plantations or as expeditionary porters. Some end up as labourers or clerks. Many have settled there and many have been born there, and a Sherpa community has long been a feature of the town. It was in Darjeeling that the British first began to hire the Sherpas as porters for their expeditions and so we earned the reputation as the best of mountain men. And now for a hundred years and more expeditions into the Himalaya have recruited us, and many are the Sherpas who in recent times have gone very high indeed on those expeditions and achieved wonderful climbs. Now we have taken to training them for full mountaineering status at our Mountaineering Institute in Darjeeling, of which I have been Director of Field Training from its beginning in 1954 until the present day. I think we have done much to raise the image of the Sherpa from its former, rather menial implication, to full recognition as a mountaineering man in his own right.

2: A TIME OF CHANGE

In *Tiger of the Snows* I described the first successful ascent of Everest in 1953 and the days of celebration that followed in Kathmandu, in Calcutta, in Delhi, in London and in Switzerland. They were very busy, very exciting days, and in some ways very difficult days, especially for me, who until then had led a life which had not prepared me for all the heroics and excitement to which I was suddenly exposed. Nor had I ever been very far from the mountains and certainly not out of India or Nepal. It was bewildering to say the least.

I also said something in the earlier book about the plan that had already been put forward that was afterwards to change my life a great deal, the plan to start a mountaineering school in Darjeeling, where I had already lived for many years and where I still live today, though in a quite different house. So although I have said that this plan eventually changed my life, it did not change it in the ways that matter—except for the many journeys abroad and the opportunity to see how other people lived in other parts of the world. For my home is still in Darjeeling, and the mountains—the very high mountains I looked upon as a boy with such awe and pleasure—are still my interest and my work. One real difference is, of course, that because of the Everest climb and the job it brought me afterwards, and the success of my first book and the journeys abroad, I have been able to give my family a much nicer home and a much better start in life than I had foreseen before the great climb. This is what gives me the greatest satisfaction; my family is my first concern and my greatest pleasure.

But what has happened in the twenty-three years that have passed since we got to the top? What has happened since we stood on the top of the mountain better known to Sherpas as Chomolungma -'Goddess-Mother of the World' some say it means, but to Sherpas 'The Mountain So High That No Bird Can Fly Over It'? We—the whole British Expedition of 1953—were the first to conquer it, after years and years of trying and the loss of quite a few lives. Many had doubted if it was worth while, worth the lives, worth the cost. Some people regarded the attempts as crazy, or at least misguided.

At times it had seemed that nobody would ever succeed. Yet today many men have stood on the top: Englishmen, New Zealanders, Scotsmen, Indians, Swiss, Americans, Chinese, Nepalis, Italians, Japanese, and many, many more will go there. Perhaps in the future it will become a routine climb for good mountaineers, now that the mysteries have been solved and climbers increase in numbers and skill, and the approach to the mountain becomes easier and easier. Once upon a time the 'ordinary' route, that is to say the route pioneered by the Swiss and successfully completed by John Hunt's team, seemed to be the very limit of climbing possibility; now not only has a large number of climbers used it, but others have taken different and far more difficult routes, like the Americans on the West Ridge in 1963 and Chris Bonnington's expedition on the nearly vertical southwest face in 1975. But make no mistake, the 'ordinary' or 'normal' route—or 'the yak trail' as some people are known to have called it disparagingly—is no easy business; it is a difficult, often dangerous and always exhausting climb, a very severe trial of a man's strength and endurance.

It may even come about one day that tourists and climbers will be carried into the Western Cwm, or to South Col, or even to the summit itself by helicopter in good weather. And a cable-car eventually to the top? I hope not. That would be horrible, but not impossible. There would be many engineering difficulties and physical ones too, especially in the matter of acclimatisation, for it takes a long time for even a fit and experienced mountaineer to get into a condition to sustain the great cold and thin air of those regions, and this fitness is usually acquired during the long march into the base and the gradually increasing altitude of the successive camps. There is already a Japanese-built hotel at Pam Laka in Khumbu, near the new Shyangboche air strip, and though not at a really great height some of the visitors without mountain experience who had been flown in have suffered a great deal of discomfort from their sudden exposure to high altitude. I believe the hotel rooms are now equipped with oxygen for use in these emergencies. I suppose a cable-car could be air-conditioned!

People ask me from time to time—not so much today, but certainly a lot during the years after the 1953 ascent if I will go to the top again, and my answer is no. I do not even want to. I have done it once, after joining in many attempts. What is the point of repeating such a climb? It can never be like the first time. I am fairly certain that I would have no great difficulty in making another ascent, despite my age, since every year of the last twenty I have many times, in my work as a climbing instructor, been going up and down great heights without any trouble, even though Everest itself has not been one of them. Besides, I have not the time for such expeditions now. My teaching duties keep me too busy.

As for the Sherpa people, already in 1953 things in the high valleys had begun to change. During the previous two or three years expeditions had passed through Solu Khumbu at first looking for a southern route to Everest and afterwards trying to reach its summit, and many Sherpas and Sherpanis had worked with these expeditions. Also, long before that, even before the last war, when Nepal was closed to tourists and climbers, Sherpas had been working as porters on expeditions to other parts of the Himalaya, on the northern routes to Everest, for instance, and up from India to the Gharwal region. I had been one such porter myself, when I first joined an Everest expedition in 1935, and travelled through Tibet to the north face of the mountain for the North Col route, and again in 1936 and 1938. I had climbed in the Gharwal as well, and in other mountains farther east.

So we knew quite a lot about westerners and their ways. They were mainly British climbers, though there were other nationalities. I suppose we became a little westernised ourselves. But it was not until Nepal was fully opened to the world a few years after the war that climbers could at last reach Everest from the south, and to do this they had to pass through Solu Khumbu and therefore through Sherpa territory. It was much the shortest approach—in fact there was no alternative, although for a long while I had continued to voice the opinion that the only approach worth trying was from the north, as I had made clear in a letter to Earl Denman in 1949—and it saved a lot of time and money compared with the old northern route, which anyway had been closed to westerners by the communist take-over.

The easier approach was one of the reasons—not the only reason—why in the 1950s the great summits were climbed one after the other. When the distances are very great and many weeks are spent in getting to a site for a base camp, lots more supplies are needed and a sense of difficulty is built up as people get tired. Even in 1953 the southern approach seemed quite long, but not nearly so long and exhausting as I remembered the long journey into Tibet. Now everything has been made even easier still.

So until then all that the people of Solu Khumbu knew of the West was what some of them, like me, knew from living in or visiting Darjeeling, and what we told our families and friends on our visits home, and what others learned from their work with expeditions. But by 1953 most of the Sherpa people, including those who had never left the valley, were becoming used to westerners, especially the Swiss, New Zealanders and British, who marched up the valleys northwards from the railhead or over the passes from Kathmandu. And they were getting to know something of what the world outside the Himalaya had to offer. Changes after that came quickly as more and more people took part in the activity. People saw and handled the food, clothing and equipment the expeditions brought with them, some of which they actually acquired when the climbers went away again and left these things behind or gave them away. Men began to leave the valley in greater numbers than before and found work in Darjeeling or Kathmandu. Many of those who left did not return. Some did return, but only as visitors, for they had made their homes elsewhere, in other towns and lands. As I had done myself.

Twenty more years have gone. Today I am over sixty. Ang Lahmu, my second wife, died of heart trouble some years ago. We had married after the death in 1944 of my first wife, Dawa Phuti, who was the mother of my daughters Pem-Pem and Nima, and of my son Nima Dorje, a very handsome boy who died in 1939 when only four years old. Ang Lahmu cared for the two girls and loved them as her own, but we had no children of this marriage and there came a time when Ang Lahmu said that I must marry again so that I might have a son. And so, not only with her agreement, but urged by her to do so, I married Daku in 1961 and soon we did have a son, and later two more sons and a daughter. Daku's full name is Dawa Phuti, exactly like my first wife's. My eldest son is Norbu Tenzing Norgay, now (1976) thirteen years old; my second is Zamling Yangdak, ten; and the youngest boy is Tenzing Damy, six. This last child was originally named Khangla Tenzing, but was renamed by the Dalai Lama during his visit to Darjeeling in the summer of 1975. In his early years Tenzing Damy was not very healthy and, according to Buddhist ideas, if a child cannot keep well he must change his name. And indeed, ever since his change of name, my son's health has improved a lot. All the children are at school now, the three boys at St Paul's, Jalapahar, while Diki Tenzing Norgay, our daughter, now eight years old, is at the Loretto Convent in Darjeeling. These schools are the best available and have all the educational traditions of the famous British schools.

Daku, who was in fact a relative of Ang Lahmu, who died in 1963, and also of my first wife, was twenty-three when we married and she came from the village of Chienyak, quite close to my own village of Thami in Khumbu. When we first met she had come down to Darjeeling for a holiday, to see and enjoy what town life had to offer, as many Sherpas do, for there is always a Sherpa population in Darjeeling, people who come down for a few weeks or months and even stay for years, or for life. Daku's parents are still alive, farmers in Khumbu and very religious people. They keep yaks and they cross-breed these yaks with cows. The male cross-breeds are very good for carrying and fetch a good price in Tibet. The female cross-breeds are good milkers, but the milk is not good for butter or cheese. The wool of the yak makes excellent carpets and there are many uses for the hides. The carpets, which are woven in their natural colours, are I think very beautiful. The yaks go over the passes from time to time to feed and of course the herdsmen go with them. There are no political difficulties in the way of these movements; you simply have to pay so much a yak for pasturing. For farming people in Khumbu there are no frontier restrictions; they go over into Tibet as and when they need and come back just as easily. Others, like myself and westerners, would be prevented.

Daku is one of six children; three boys and three girls. Two of her brothers are in Darjeeling and one still lives with the old people. Her two sisters are both married, one living in Kathmandu and the other in Namche Bazar, on the Everest route. Before our first child was born Daku did quite a lot of mountaineering with me in Sikkim, where she would accompany me to the Institute's training grounds; since then she has climbed also in America and in North Wales and has taken the ladies' course of the Institute at both the basic and advanced levels. She is a good mountaineer, perfectly safe, and she enjoys climbing. She has a lot of confidence. She also occasionally leads tours in Sikkim and Nepal and on those journeys she may be away for as long as three weeks at a time. Her parties have been mixed, men and women; one of them was to the sacred lake of Gosainkund at a height of 16,000 feet in north Nepal, created, it is said, by the Lord Shiva himself. It is most beautiful and is thought to feed the Kumbestwar Pond in Patan by a long underground river.

My greatest wish for these four children, as it was for Nima and Pem-Pem, who are both married now and out in the world and no longer need my help, is that they shall have the best possible start in life that I can give them. This is expensive and my own earnings could not have paid for it all, but the generosity of others has made it possible and I am grateful.

Meanwhile there are a lot of people dependent upon me, people whom I had not expected. For when I was young, long before the Everest climbs, I was quite out of touch with relatives other than my immediate family and not much even with some of them. After I came to Darjeeling I was away from my home village for fifteen years and saw nothing of them; for communication in those days was little and difficult, and for people who cannot write, to keep contact is almost impossible. But after the ascent of Everest and all the fame and publicity along they came, brothers and sisters, cousins, aunts, uncles, nephews, in-laws and all sorts of relatives I had never seen or heard of before. They all came and said, I am your cousin so-and-so, I am your uncle so-and-so, I am your brother-in-law, I am your aunt, and so on. They settled on me one after the other, and I had to house and look after them. What else could I do? It was, after all, my duty.

My home in Darjeeling was fairly small, but comfortable, and it was quiet. But not for long. Very soon I had to enlarge it and it was full and noisy all the time. Because I was famous they thought I was rich. I was not, and I am not rich today. You do not make a lot of money by climbing a mountain, and I had rightly turned down a lot of commercial offers because of their difficult complications. Yet I was able to manage and I did what I thought was my duty. Most of these people were quite ungrateful. They never seemed satisfied, and I do not like them. Some are with me still. It was very difficult. It still is.

However, my own family originally included three sisters, two older than me: Kipa, who is no more, and Takchu, who is still alive. But the third and younger sister, Sonam Doma, used to look after my land for me in the Solu Khumbu valley, and in 1955 came down to Darjeeling and stayed with me for a few months. Later she lived for a while in Phulbari near Jaynagar in India, a very hot place indeed, and she died of heat stroke, leaving four girls and a boy. The husband, after her death, took to drink, so I accepted responsibility for the children and in 1956 brought them into my home. The four girls are still with me, though one has now married, but the son, who for a while worked in the Indo-Tibetan Border Police, is now dead. I count them all as part of my own big family and I am very fond of them. The girls are named Ang Phuti, Ang Neme, Pem Phuti and Yangzey.

I was always a traveller in a certain sense. Long ago, when I was a young Sherpa porter, I was frequently away from home. At eighteen I had left Khumbu to find a living in the town, and then, after I was married, I was often on expeditions. I was young and ambitious, and I had to earn a living anyway, and that was not easy in those days. I saw my wife and babies when there was no climbing to be done. My long absences must have been disappointing for both Dawa Phuti and Ang Lahmu, but that is what Sherpa wives have to put up with. Then came the succession of long expeditions, and then, after Everest had at last been climbed, the travelling increased and, following several European journeys, it took me all over the world. In the past twenty years I have seen much of western Europe, also of America, Russia, New Zealand, Australia, a great deal of India and some of the Far East. I am always in the air going somewhere. Very long journeys many of them and on some I am lucky to have had Daku with me. My elder daughters have travelled far too, especially Nima, who has lived in many distant lands. Both Pem-Pem and Nima are married and have families of their own; Pem-Pem married a Sherpa in government service in Darjeeling and has two sons and a daughter and is matron now at St Paul's school where my boys are being educated.

And so, although I still live in Darjeeling, I seem to have come a long way from my Khumbu beginnings. My own success, the things I have done and the fame that came with them, have themselves played an unavoidable part in changing the life of my native valley. That change has not been altogether good, and for this I have to accept a little responsibility. I certainly had not foreseen such changes as a consequence of the conquest of Everest. Yet because of it I had been enabled to live very comfortably by Sherpa standards and to go places Sherpa people had never dreamed of before. I became famous and met famous people and secured a good living. It was natural that other Sherpas should wish to do the same, and in fact some who followed after me have done very well indeed. And so, if I am happy about my own success, if I am happy about my work and my family life far away from the valley where I was born, I am saddened a little by the changes that have overtaken the Himalayan people in recent years.

I ask myself: is it good that we Sherpas are deserting our traditional ways, that we have come to accept the ways of the West, that we are forgetting our own religion and even our own language? Of course, many of the things brought to the Sherpas by westerners have included very great benefits, not the least being real medical help where none was ever available before, also a higher standard of living, a good education and opportunities to move about. Life in Solu Khumbu when I was young was really poor; real sickness mostly meant great suffering and often death; diseases like smallpox raged unchecked and swept people away; sometimes the crops failed and in a land where there was never more than enough food that could mean disaster, with hunger and starvation. As for education, even today I cannot read or write and I often wish I could, since to produce a book like this I have to rely on my memory entirely and on other people to do the actual writing. And then it has to be read to me afterwards to make sure it is right. My children, however, can all read and write, and so can most young Sherpas today—Hillary and his men have built a school even in my own native village of Thami—but not in their own Sherpa language. For me it was already too late at the time of Everest, up till when it had not mattered; though it has been embarrassing at times since, I think it would be too difficult at my present age to try and start.

In the business of being absorbed into modern life the Sherpas' traditional ways, Buddhist by religion and Tibetan outwardly, all those things that gave the Sherpas their special strength and difference, have been wasting away, even the language itself. The children are taught Nepali or English, and many of them know no Sherpa, and I suppose that soon, as a way of speaking and thinking, it will disappear completely, especially as it has no written form and therefore no records. Once it has gone it can never again be revived. Yet when the Swiss came to Namche Bazar in 1953 a teacher was employed there to teach the children Nepali; all they knew was Tibetan!

I am told that this would have happened anyway one day, with or without the conquest of Everest, with or without Tenzing; someone else would have done what I have done, and the older ways are breaking down all over the world in places that were once remote and are remote no longer. The Sherpas could not have stayed apart from the rest of the world for ever. But it is a fact that in Solu Khumbu a special way of life is dying, and with it a language and a culture, and that cannot be a good thing. It is certainly a sad thing. I often wonder about this: you bring to a people a new way of life and a better standard of living, you give them schools and hospitals, all of which is good, but at the same time you tear them up from their roots, and I cannot think that this can be good too. I wonder if and when they will grow new roots and what they will be like. In days gone by no Sherpa child would go begging; now the cry of 'baksheesh' is heard where the tourists pass by on their way up the valley.

Myself, I still speak Sherpa and I am a Buddhist and still hold to the Buddhist faith and tradition. In that sense I am a religious man, though I am not one for forms and ceremonies. Yet in my Darjeeling home I have a room where we pray—you of the West would call it a chapel—and on the walls are beautiful thankas, those highly-coloured holy picture-scrolls from Tibet. It is very peaceful there and from its window you can look out on the lovely face of Kangchenjunga, the finest mountain scene, I think, in the whole world.

3: A NEW CAREER

For me, however, a new life began when we returned from the mountains in June 1953. All sorts of propositions were made to me about my future. There were attempts to drag me into a political life, but Sir John Hunt had warned against these moves and I avoided politically-minded people as far as I could. Newspaper men especially, but others too, tried to drag me into a sort of East-West confrontation and to set me up as the hero of Asia. This was difficult, but in time it all died down.

Even as soon as we had reached Kathmandu I had been approached by an Indian film star with a plan for getting me into the film world, and he tried to tempt me with a very large sum of money. To a man as poor as I was, it certainly was a temptation. But John Hunt's advice to stick to mountaineering was already deeply fixed in my mind, and when I discussed the proposition later with Pandit Jawaharlal Nehru in Delhi it was not so hard to decide to decline the offer and Panditji was delighted at my decision.

In Calcutta there was a lot of excitement and many official receptions; it was during this time that Dr B. C. Roy, the Chief Minister for West Bengal, brought up again for discussion the idea of establishing an Indian school of mountaineering, an idea that had first been mooted by my friend Robi Mitra. Dr Roy asked the members of the expedition what they thought of the plan and all of them, including their leader, strongly recommended that a start should be made as soon as possible. And there the matter was left for the time being, for these days were very busy indeed.

There were more receptions as we went from Calcutta to Delhi—where I met Pandit Nehru, who was very kind and helpful to me and gave me much advice, which I have tried to follow carefully through the years. Pandit Nehru became a close friend and I saw him many times afterwards, and he would never mind at all when I brought my problems to him. And from Delhi we moved on to Karachi, Rome, Zurich and London, where we stayed for many days and were presented to Queen Elizabeth and the Duke of Edinburgh and received our medals and awards. All this was a great honour to me and my family—Ang Lahmu and my two daughters were with me—and to my Sherpa comrades of Everest and the whole Sherpa people, which made me very happy.

When all the receptions and dinners and speeches were over and all the members of the expedition had gone back to their homes, I went with my family and my friend Lhakpa Tschering to Switzerland to see my companions of the Swiss expedition to Everest of the year before, the expedition that had explored the great ice-fall which was almost unknown until then—only Eric Shipton and friends had looked at it closely—and the route to South Col and the summit, and had come so near to success. That was when Raymond Lambert and I were high on the South Ridge of the mountain and hoping to reach the top in the morning. That night we had realised that the fierce wind that was already blowing could cost us our lives if it continued, yet we went on up. We spent that terrible night beating and rubbing each other in the effort to keep ourselves warm and survive. That *terrible* Everest wind! Terrible! Yet we did try when morning came and for five hours, in raging wind and snow, we struggled up another 650 feet. Five hours for 650 feet—130 feet an hour!—and then, at 28,250 feet, the nearest that man had ever got to the top—unless Mallory and Irvine had got there before they disappeared—we were forced to decide to retreat. We had given everything we knew and all our strength, but it was not enough. We descended in silence, knowing this had been our last chance. Such experiences bring men very close together.

All this had taken place little more than a year before and the sadness of that defeat, in spite of the success I had had in the interval, was very strong when I met Raymond again in Switzerland in the summer of 1953. I spent some enjoyable days in Geneva before we went on to Zurich for a reception at which Carl Weber and Ernst Feuz of the Swiss Foundation for Alpine Research were present, as well as Dr Roy, who was then in Switzerland for treatment for eye trouble. After the reception, at the end of July, the subject of the Indian mountaineering school was raised and discussed once more. Dr Roy and myself were present at the discussions.

Our Swiss friends were much in favour of the scheme and offered to help in any way they could. A 'primary draft' of the scheme was laid out, fixing the general lines on which the school could be created and conducted. It was also decided at this time that I should be in charge of field training at the school and that its headquarters should be in Darjeeling, not for any reason but that it is a good mountain centre with a mountaineering tradition, has fairly good communications, is well-provided with services and is very close to high mountains where the school's students would be able to find plenty of climbing terrain of every variety. It is also quite close to the Sherpa homeland, with plenty of Sherpas actually living in the town.

Darjeeling is beautifully situated. I have lived there now for over forty years. At first I lived in the Toong Soong Busti area, where most Tibetans in Darjeeling have their homes, a densely populated district along from the market square on the side of a hill. Not until the final Everest climb did I acquire a bigger and better home on the Tonga Road, quite a long way from Toong Soong Busti, which I called 'Ghang-La', meaning 'Snowy Pass'; it is the name also of a pilgrimage monastery close to the mountain Makalu in Nepal and the place where I was born. It is my family or clan name, too, so far as such things exist, because as a reward for good service in the army of Gyalbo Khung, long ago, my ancestors were given land at that spot. In Toong Soong Busti the houses we Sherpas lived in were long wooden shacks with tin roofs for the most part; two or three families might live in one shack and a whole family might share one room. We were continuously in and out of each others' quarters and we were a close and happy community. To the outsider it might appear very confined and confusing, with its crowded and numerous alleys and its almost strict tribal background; but in fact we all knew what everyone else was doing and where and how to find anyone when necessary; communication was very quick and easy. This is how I lived with my first wife, who also came from Solu Khumbu, and like me was of Tibetan origin, but we were young and fairly content with our lives.

'Ghang-La' is a very different sort of house, tall, with many rooms, built in a traditional style and quite a bit of land of its own, on a very steeply sloping site in full view of Kangchenjunga. The interior is entirely Tibetan. In one room I keep an old Tibetan chest and in it are all my medals and trophies, an extraordinary collection which never ceases to surprise me whenever I lift the lid to show the contents to some special visitor.

After the ascent of Everest a lot of publicity was made with a view to building me a new house, although I already had one that was quite good and big enough. A newspaper actually offered house-building materials like cement, glass, wood and so forth. Another newspaper collected a great sum of money for the same purpose. I did not know what to do and was not at all prepared to accept these offers. So once again I went to Pandit Nehru for advice, and he said: 'Look, Tenzing. It is nice that people have shown affection and have collected such a handsome sum of money. No doubt they are all grateful to you. But the money collected in this way is a donation from the people. Suppose you use it for a house. When you grow old people will not hesitate to say that your house was built by public donation. You would not like them to say that. You have a house already; why not repair it and make it attractive? So do not accept this money. '

How right Panditji was! But as the newspaper had collected a good sum of money and my reluctance to accept it made them unhappy, to give them a little satisfaction, and rather against my will, I agreed to take a small part of it, and the rest I put into a Sherpa Trust Fund of which I am still the president. The fund was created for the welfare of Sherpas, and sixteen of those who had been on the expedition to the South Pole each received grants from the fund, which also gives assistance to the poor and needy members of the Sherpa community, the widows, the education of Sherpa children and the medical expenses of Sherpas and their families. The fund still exists today.

'Ghang-La' stands where the tourists come to see the famous view of Kangchenjunga -besides the many uninvited people who come to look at me. Some of these have caused a lot of trouble at times, invading both the house and the garden. To stop them I had to get the help of the police, but this was expensive and eventually my Tibetan mastiff solved the problem. He is a fierce animal and people take no chances. He is better than all the police put together.

But to return to Darjeeling. It was originally a holiday resort standing at 7,000 feet, where some of the world's highest mountains seem quite close, especially Kangchenjunga, the third highest on earth and the most majestic, flanked on either side by other huge mountains, but small enough by comparison to set the big one off. Kangchenjunga is only 850 feet less in height than Everest and was not climbed until two years after Everest, and then by a British expedition. It is a region of terrible winds and huge avalanches, but the great covering of snow is what makes it so beautiful, at dawn especially, seen from the Darjeeling hills. I never tire of watching it, as I did when I first arrived in the town: rose-red in the first light of morning, and when the weather is clear by day rising huge and brilliantly white, high in the sky, fifty miles away. As night falls it looks thin and cold, but still enormous, beyond the valleys that are already filled with darkness, as if it did not belong to the earth at all. Unfortunately, the weather is not always helpful and many have come to see this magnificent view and found nothing but cloud. That is the way with mountains.

Many other great mountains can be seen from Darjeeling, and are even nearer than Kangchenjunga: Jannu, Kabru, Koktang, Ratong, Siniolchu and Simbhu, all close and above 20,000 feet high. Amongst them could be some excellent training grounds for the school and I had already had some climbing experience amongst them.

Four hours' drive from the town, but still within the District, is a mountain called Sandakphu, about 12,000 feet high, from which there is another fine view that includes Everest itself, Makalu, Lhotse, Nuptse and Chomolhari in faraway Tibet.

Darjeeling is a good town to live in. It has its old quarters, with temples, bazaars, narrow streets, old houses and colourful crowds, and shops where absolutely anything can be bought. On the hill above are the homes that were built by the English in their own style, though few Englishmen or Europeans live there now, and the homes of rich Indians, hotels, administrative buildings and modern-style stores. Darjeeling has not changed much with the years, except that there are many more people, and I was happy that the school was to be situated there; the town could provide everything such an institution and its students might need and we could surely find a good site for our headquarters, with excellent training areas within easy reach. These were questions that were to be settled soon.

So these decisions were taken in Zurich in July 1953, only a few weeks after I had stood on the top of Everest. So much seemed to have happened in so short a time! As part of the plan, the Swiss Foundation said that I must come back to Switzerland and go through the regular training course for Swiss mountain guides, followed by additional training under Dr Glatthard at his climbing school at Rosenlaui in the Bernese Oberland. The idea was that in the company of alpine guides I could acquire the same degree of skill and technical knowledge that permits them to take climbers out on the most difficult of their own mountains. At Dr Glatthard's school it would be a matter of even more intensive training on the same lines. I should be in Switzerland for three months altogether and, starting a little later than myself, six selected Sherpas would join me at Rosenlaui for an instructional course of six weeks. It was thought that, after my longer training, I should be able to complete the training of the Sherpas when we all got back to the Himalaya.

The Swiss also promised to help us with equipment, not only for us Sherpas while training but also for the school when it had been set up. Finally, it was arranged that Dr Glatthard himself would come out to Darjeeling in the autumn to survey the area and make recommendations as to where the headquarters should be built and where the training area should be.

Then Dr Roy and I went back to India with the main plans for the school well advanced, though there were many problems still to solve. Dr Roy took the plans to Nehru, who approved them but said that he thought we might have difficulty in finding enough students to make the school worth while. But Dr Roy replied that he saw nothing to worry about; we should make a start and see how things went. As it happened, the very next year after this discussion about our school I travelled through many parts of India on a lecture tour to show films of the mountains and to promote the idea of mountaineering amongst Indian people, to most of whom it had meant nothing until then. As a result I managed to collect eighteen students for the first course in 1954. Now, of course, we have many, many more every year.

The next problem was money. We had to have a headquarters building, an organisation and staff, and though these could be small to start with, if we were to get anywhere at all they would soon have to be much bigger. But Dr Roy was a strong man and he solved this problem too. The school was to be a government institution, financed partly by the Central Government and partly by the Government of West Bengal, with contributions also from the Ministry of Defence, which would send us some students from among the men who were training for mountain warfare. Also, we persuaded a certain number of rich industrialists and companies to give us money and soon our immediate financial problems were settled.

This is how the Himalayan Mountaineering Institute—HMI we call it amongst ourselves—came into existence. All its staff, myself included, became salaried teachers from the start because the Institute was part of the educational system of the State, just like any other school or the universities.

And this is how the herd-boy from Solu Khumbu, who watched his father's yaks on the high pastures within sight of the Everest range and dreamed that he might one day get to the top, who became eventually a mountain porter carrying the loads of other climbers to the mountains he loved, finally found himself a teacher of climbers, and for another twenty years and more helped other men to gain the skills and confidence to climb those mountains too. It seems to me now to have been a long and strange journey, but always a happy one and full of reward.

4: THE HIMALAYAN MOUNTAINEERING INSTITUTE

The plan which had been developed in Zurich and which Dr Roy and Pandit Nehru were considering was for a basic course which would serve not only to introduce mountaineering to Indian people as a sport and an adventure, but just as much to show them the mountains and their beauties and to bring them into touch with the mountain people—the Sherpas for instance, but other Himalayan communities as well. The Institute would teach its students the history of the Himalayan region and explain the geography and geology, meteorology and botany of the mountains. Students would learn also about the other mountain ranges of the world and the history of mountain exploration and climbing, all of course at an elementary level, and they would have instruction in hygiene and fitness, diet and nutrition, and so on.

Further, the Swiss Foundation, which was helping us in such a practical way, had their own idea about the future of the Sherpa people. They held that the Sherpas had usually been considered until then as being fit to do the bulk of the hard work—the 'donkey-work'—of an expedition without being regarded as the social equals of the climbers. So it was one of their aims to improve the professional standing of Sherpas, and Sherpa training has ever since the start been a strong part of our programme. We have in fact turned out a remarkable number of very skilled men from our regular Sherpa intake. This question apart, however, the Institute's hope and intention was to give the young people of India a love and understanding of mountain life; it was to be a cultural as well as a sporting activity.

Now as I have already said, Pandit Nehru had been doubtful if we could find enough students, but Dr Roy had been very confident, and at first they were recruited from the Army, the Police, the Scouts; and soon they came from all parts of India, some as private persons, including those who had been encouraged to do so by my lecture tour. Panditji had said to me: 'We will start the Himalayan Mountaineering Institute. You will be in charge as Director of Field Training. You have climbed the highest mountain in the world. Your name is Tenzing. Now you will make a thousand Tenzings. You will train as many as possible. ' A very big order to carry out!

In charge of administration at the Institute, its Principal in fact, was Major N. D. Jayal, 'Nandu', whom I had already known for many years in mountaineering activity. At that time he was probably the only fully accomplished mountaineer in India. In 1958 he died of pneumonia during an expedition to the summit of Cho Oyu, and Indian mountaineering lost a very great man. During his career he succeeded in many great and difficult ascents. Nandu's successor was Brigadier Gyan Singh and he was succeeded in turn by Commander Kohli.

Arnold Glatthard arrived in India from Rosenlaui in the middle of

October, and with Major Jayal and myself, with a few Sherpas, made a trek into Sikkim to reconnoitre the region east of the Kangchenjunga chain to discover a suitable place for our training area, but not before exploring Darjeeling itself in search of the best possible site for the headquarters.

Though there are many fine mountains quite close to the town they are not at all suitable for serious mountain instruction, so the area we carefully surveyed lay north of Darjeeling in the neighbourhood of Ratong (21,904 feet) and Kabru (24,063 feet), part of a high range forming the frontiers of Sikkim and Nepal. These were the very mountains which the Swiss climber, Georg Frey, had been exploring with me in 1951 when he slipped and plunged to his death on Kang Peak, not a very high mountain but an impressive one that had not until then been climbed by anyone. Frey was a very good climber and his accident took me by surprise. We were not roped, it is true, but the rope was not really necessary for an experienced man like Frey, the going was not at all difficult and the slope not steep. I had actually stopped to put on crampons and had suggested to Frey that he might do so too, but he did not think so. When he fell a little later I just could not believe it. I reached out to catch him as he passed; it was an instinctive move and not very hopeful. For he was going by too fast. This was the first and only fatal fall in which I have been closely involved and the experience was deeply shocking. In none of my climbs since then, on Everest with both the Swiss and the British, was there an accident of this kind, and during the whole twenty years of training students of the Institute we are lucky to have had no fatal fall.

About six or seven miles short of the valley head and the tongue of the East Ratong Glacier, on what we have called the Kabur Saddle, we fixed the site of the base from which beginners would work. It stands at about 14,700 feet, some 1,500 feet above the hamlet of Dzongri. It is quite close to really high terrain and provides our students with access to every kind of climbing, rock and ice, easy and difficult. The summit of Kabur itself is 15,780 feet high, that is to say, almost the same height as Mont Blanc, the highest mountain of the European Alps. It rises above the camp and on its northward-stretching ridge are excellent areas for rock-climbing, while even farther along the ridge and higher still there is a region of snow and ice reaching up to 18,000 feet for exercise on that sort of terrain. At the head of the valley a further site was selected as a base for advanced students, close to a whole group of summits, including Ratong and Kabru (not to be confused with Kabur), one of them over 24,000 feet high. There is also a third camp-site in a side valley below Koktang (20,167 feet), suitable for intermediate students if required. At first Dr Glatthard had recommended that we should build a proper alpine-style hut at Kabur Saddle, but we have never done so because we regard the pitching and taking down of tents, sleeping under canvas and keeping tents in order all as part of the business of an expedition, something every mountaineering student should learn to do under all conditions.

There was a choice of routes between Darjeeling and our bases. One ran along the border between Sikkim and Nepal through Sandakphu and Tikipchu, but this takes a few days longer than the 'Sikkim' route through Pemayongtse, farther inside Sikkim's territory. Dr Glatthard favoured the latter because it would leave the students more time for their training.

These were our Swiss friend's main conclusions and he gave them to Dr Roy when he got back to Calcutta late in November, and to the Swiss Foundation on his return to Zurich. The Swiss discussed the recommendations and then laid out a whole plan of how the Institute should be organised, how and where it should be accommodated, the number of personnel and their duties, the quantity and nature of supplies and equipment down to the least detail, the general principles of its teaching—everything we needed to know in order to get the Institute together quickly and effectively. It was a wonderfully detailed document, which was promptly passed to Calcutta, and Calcutta took action quickly. For it was our hope to open HMI in the autumn of 1954 in time for the Himalayan climbing season, after the monsoon is over and the skies clear to give a longish spell of quiet weather. Beginning with November and lasting till early February, this can be a very beautiful time of the year in the Himalaya, with cloudless skies, little wind and no great heat.

Before that time arrived I had to get my own training finished. The Swiss had now definitely decided to bring me back to the Alps for a course of training with their own candidates for an alpine guide's certificate. In the summer of 1954, therefore, I travelled back to Europe and from 4 to 27 June, with the help of the Swiss Alpine Club and the cantonal authorities of Valais, Major Jayal and I took part in the guide's course at Champex, a pretty lakeside village at the Swiss end of the Mont Blanc range, with high and beautiful mountains all around. There were about forty or fifty Swiss candidates for the certificate.

Naturally, there were difficulties, and language was one of them. I could not speak or understand German; the Swiss could certainly not speak or understand Hindi or Nepali or Sherpa! What we had in common was a little English, and my English in those days was not even as good as it is today. So the best I could do most of the time was just watch and follow. Then again, the Swiss seemed to have the idea that I was a sort of beginner in climbing; this was because, I suppose, all the other candidates had been through proper, systematic courses of instruction before they had reached candidate's level, which is what I had not done, although I had climbed a very great deal in all conditions and for many years, and had learned much about climbing techniques on the expeditions in which I had taken part. Admittedly, my experience of rock-climbing was small and in Switzerland there was quite a lot of rock to tackle. Faced with these difficulties this was not a very easy time. It was certainly a very useful one.

On leaving Champex, Jayal and I went on to Rosenlaui, where the six Sherpas I had chosen for special training before I left Darjeeling joined us at Dr Glatthard's school of mountaineering. Two of them had been with me on Everest the previous year: Da Namgyal and Ang Tempa. Two were already well-known and experienced climbers in the Himalaya: Ang Tharkay and Gyalzen Mikcha. The remaining two were my own nephews, Nwang Gombu and Nwang Topgya. A lot will be heard of Gombu later, for since those days he has become a very great mountaineer indeed; he, too, was in the British 1953 expedition.

At Rosenlaui, a grassy alp among lovely forests on the eastern side of the Grosse Scheideck, not far from Grindelwald, with a view of many fine mountains—like the Wetterhorn and the Wellhorn—we stayed from 19 July till 6 September and went through another period of intensive training and gained a lot of experience on every kind of mountain terrain.

After general training and a refresher course in ropework: how to tie the various knots and what their purposes are, followed by rope practice on both rock and ice with parties of different numbers, the six Sherpas and Jayal and I received detailed instruction in ice craft and all kinds of step-cutting—straight up a slope, diagonally across it, zigzagging—the use of crampons and so on. We had instruction, too, in belaying under all sorts of conditions, also in the use of every kind of modern equipment like ice-pitons and ice-pipes, and how to use ice-blocks for self-belaying. We worked also at roping-down on ice and snow and rock, at crossing glacier crevasses, and all kinds of snow techniques. We learned about cornices and avalanches and what to do about them, and we took instruction on rescue work in all sorts of circumstances. It was exceedingly detailed and most systematic and I cannot list here all the things we were asked to do. And it was very strenuous too. Dr Glatthard said that his method of training was like what a mother chamois teaches her young, so that everything comes naturally and spontaneously when the need arises.

We Sherpas had to learn all these things not only for our own sakes; we had to know and understand them so well that we could later pass our knowledge on to the students of HMI back in the Himalaya, so that they in their turn might become skilled and safe in the mountains. In the course of this instruction, some of which was done quite close to the school at Rosenlaui, we also made a number of rock and ice climbs in the Bernese Oberland where we could make full use of what we had learnt: the Wellhorn, Kingspitz, Simmelistock, Gelmerhorn, Gespaltenhorn and Dosenhorn, and also a number of snow climbs, like the Wetterhorn, Monch, Jungfrau, Fiescherhorn, Finsteraarhorn, and others, all first-class climbs that gave us practice in all the things we had been taught. We lived in the alpine club huts as we passed from one mountain to another, as well as in Dr Glatthard's headquarters at Rosenlaui.

It may seem strange to readers of my earlier book that I who had done so much mountaineering already during the previous twenty years, and who had not only stood on top of the world's highest mountain but had climbed more difficult summits than that (like Nanda Devi in 1951) should have to go to school again and learn the facts of mountaineering. It is certainly true that many of the things we had to do in Champex and Rosenlaui I had already been doing for a long time on the expeditions I had worked with in the Himalaya, and under worse climatic conditions than those of Switzerland, where we were always within close reach of shelter and help. But there were quite a lot of things that were new to me, and anyway it was a good thing to learn things systematically and to understand why they are done and when, in a way that we could pass on to others. It is one thing to pick things up as you go along with an expedition and quite another thing to bring all these techniques together as a complete system ready for immediate use when required. Also, if we were going to teach other people we had to know the business completely.

Actually, I had not until then had a lot of experience of rock climbing, since my Himalayan climbing had been almost wholly on ice and snow. So I had to have a lot more practice in that field. Also, mountaineering methods are changing and developing all the time and new items of equipment are constantly appearing. In Switzerland we became familiar with these and saw them in action. Today, at our training quarters in Sikkim, we use the same equipment and show our students how to use it. The weather in the Alps that summer was not good, but even so we were able to cover the course as planned. Dr Glatthard spoke to us always in English and we could all understand him clearly, so there were no language difficulties as at Champex. At Rosenlaui we were not isolated from other climbers; we mixed with them all. There was a simple mountain atmosphere about the school which we much enjoyed, and in the Swiss mountains I felt quite at home, sometimes as if I were back in the Himalaya, except that they were not so high or so big, nor were the distances so great. I enjoy the company of Swiss climbers; I suppose because they are a mountain people too, we have much in common. I like their very real friendliness and their unpretentious ways. I like their style of climbing, too, as compared with what I have seen of the American style, which often works with a very long rope that I personally find disconcerting, I like the short rope technique of the Alps; I find it much safer. With the long rope there is a long run-out if there is a slip, and the eventual jerk can be very dangerous for both climbers. When I was on Mount Rainier and later on Mount Hood in the western United States, I would find myself sometimes quite alone, watching the rope above run right out of sight. I like to have my climbing comrade always fairly close within view, whether I lead or am being led; only that way can it be said that there is reasonable security.

When our Swiss training ended we returned to Darjeeling, where the official opening of the Institute by Pandit Nehru took place on 4 November 1954. To begin with the staff consisted of Major Jayal as Principal and myself as Director of

Field Training, six Sherpa instructors, a storekeeper and four or five headquarters personnel. At that time we had no real headquarters building, only a small, rented temporary office, yet it was beautifully located about two miles from the town. Later we moved to a fine hill-top site at Birch Hill, above St Joseph's College, where the permanent headquarters were built to our own requirements. This is the site that Dr Glatthard had recommended, with a wonderful view of the mountains—Kanchenjunga and the Sikkim Himalaya. A really beautiful place; one of the best in all Darjeeling. Dr Roy had said we could choose anywhere we liked; whatever the cost, the money would be found. As it happened, the site was public property anyway—actually a picnic place—so no one was inconvenienced by its appro-pria-tion. It has plenty of open space and trees around and now, attached to the Institute, there is a Himalayan Zoo, where we even have twelve Siberian tigers, all born there, the descendants of two that were given by Mr Khrushchev to Pandit Nehru. We also have yaks, Himalayan bears, many Himalayan birds, but no monkeys, only animals special to our mountains. Although the immediate surroundings provide no real facilities for teaching or practising climbing, the headquarters has plenty of space for basic physical training and camping exercises, which are all necessary to expeditionary work. Today it has living quarters for both instructors and students, an equipment wing in which all the material needed for training is kept and where we can even make some to our own design; also a medical wing, including a research department where we can make investigations into the effects of altitude on heart and lungs, and so on, a museum, a lecture hall and cinema, a library, classrooms—everything. It even has a particularly powerful telescope which was once the property of Adolf Hitler. The Institute's headquarters took a year to build; the architect was American; it is built mainly of concrete and is of wholly modern design.

The Swiss Foundation gave us a lot of modern equipment so that we could start our training programme unhindered. They provided twenty-five sets of every-thing the student would need: tents, ice-axes, crampons, boots, gloves, downfilled clothing, sleeping bags, back-packs, ropes, pitons and other such implements, and even kitchen ware. Everything, in fact, except the food!

We had only eighteen students at the start, some paid for by the services that sponsored them, and a few private students who paid for themselves. The fees were only Rs 400—about £25—for everything, accommodation at the Institute and in the mountains, the loan of clothing and equipment, food and tuition and medical care, everything for six weeks. And the fees today, more than twenty years later, are exactly the same. All the students—or their sponsors—pay the same; there is no dif-ferentiation for any reason, whether for advanced or basic training, even though advanced students actually spend longer in the field. Of course, the true cost must be several times what is charged, but the authorities make up the difference.

Our students come from many different parts of India. Most of them have never before seen a mountain, certainly nothing like the Himalaya. Most have never seen snow, and begin the training with a fear of heights; quite a few suffer nausea or vertigo, but it is good to see how well they tackle the course nevertheless and soon overcome these difficulties and go away at the end pleased with the idea of returning. The majority come from the cities, which are in the plains, and often they are not used to open spaces; men from Madras, Bombay, Calcutta or Delhi and even from the far south of India. They come straight up to Darjeeling and feel the effects of altitude for the first time in their lives. So we keep them there for a week to get used to things and acclimatise a little, also to undergo a complete and strict medical investigation to make sure they are fit for strenuous exercise at this or even greater heights.

Apart from all the equipment they had provided and the instructor training, the Swiss had also drawn up for us a fully detailed 'outline of a course' which they recommended we should follow. This included a full syllabus of preliminary theoretical studies in meteorology, geology, cartography, geography, photography, mountain history and general hygiene. These studies, apart from general physical training, are what the men occupy themselves with during that preliminary week at Darjeeling. There are lectures and discussions on all related subjects, as well as plenty of time for students to familiarise themselves with their mountain clothing and personal equipment. There are two hours each day for elementary training in rock-climbing among the easy rocks of the neighbourhood. Then we load them up with thirty-five pounds of pack each and walk them up and down the local hills for about five or six miles at a time. All this while I watch them very carefully to see if their reactions suggest they are suitable or not for training as mountaineers and for living and working at high altitudes. For even at 7,000 feet, to carry a pack of thirty-five pounds is quite a trial if you have never done it before, and on a full-scale expedition each of them would have to carry a load of far greater weight than that, and with even thinner air to breathe.

There are many other things to be done in that first week. Especially fitting the students with their mountain boots almost certainly, for the beginners, for the very first time in their lives. Many have never even worn ordinary heavy footwear and they have to get used to the weight and feel of them. We have to ensure the fit is perfect and that no blisters are likely to develop, for a blister could spoil the whole course and a bad case could not possibly start on the eight-day march to base camp which begins a few days later. During that march, however, students wear lighter, canvas footwear with rubber soles and only put on their boots for the rock and ice.

We provide the students with all their personal equipment: boots, climbing pants, socks, gloves, windproof jacket and trousers, down clothing, sleeping bags—the lot.

5: THE MAKING OF A MOUNTAINEER

The march to base camp, which lasts eight days, is all part of the basic training of a student mountaineer. Today you could travel half-way to the camp by jeep, but we do not allow it; the students must know how to deal with all possible eventualities, like crossing rivers if bridges have been washed away, with floods and broken tracks, and the march is in any case a part of the toughening process. It also provides an opportunity to explain the landscape to our students, as well as the history and traditions of the area.

On each working day we reckon to cover from twelve to fifteen miles. The students carry all their own equipment, that is to say everything except tents and food, for the larger tents, once camp has been established, remain in position for the rest of the season until the course is over. Each man carries his own sleeping-bag, climbing gear and personal effects, which make a total weight of about sixty pounds, and is no more than the normal load for a porter on any expedition. To carry such a pack for eight days on mountain territory is an essential part of the experience, for anyone, climber or Sherpa, amateur or professional, has to carry as much in any part of the mountain world until he reaches his base. Except excursionists, of course.

Acclimatisation is carefully planned. First we take our students up to 10,000 feet—about 3,000 feet higher than Darjeeling itself, and there we stay for a whole day to get them accustomed to the altitude. There is a doctor with the party always, and he can see just how each man responds to altitude and effort. This doctor is usually an army man seconded to the Institute temporarily. During the day's halt we do not rest; the men are given plenty of up-hill walking and some rock-climbing experience. There are lectures to attend also; in fact, all the way to base I am talking to the students singly or in groups about their problems.

When we get moving again we go up to 12,000 feet for a two-day halt, which takes the acclimatisation process a stage further. Finally we reach base camp at nearly 15,000 feet, where we stay for two weeks, climbing on rock and ice and snow in the neighbouring mountains, and when that is over we march back to Darjeeling. During the whole thirty days there is much for the beginner to learn, especially in matters of camp hygiene, upkeep of the outfit (e. g. daily cleaning and drying of mattresses, sleeping bags and clothing), preparation of camp-sites, erection and breaking of camp, construction of camp-kitchens, and a host of other such things. A man also learns to accommodate himself to things he has not experienced before, like dehydration at high altitude, and even temperamental changes which are not unusual. He should, by the time he reaches base, have learnt how to adjust himself to the needs of the team.

The approach march is one of great beauty. The party is very big and sets out at the cool morning hour of seven. It usually consists of fifty students for the basic course and forty advanced students who, together with nine instructors and more than 200 porters, makes a column of 300 men all moving up together.

The first day takes us to Singla, ten miles from the River Rangeet which divides India from Sikkim. This stage is easy and the students usually hurry along through the tea gardens with great enthusiasm. The colourfully-dressed hill girls, busy picking, never miss an opportunity to joke and chatter with the men, and on its way our caravan passes many groups of Sikkimese peasants taking their fruit, vegetables, poultry and eggs to market in Darjeeling.

From Singla, which is on the Indian side of the border, we cross into Sikkim over a suspension bridge. The one now in use is a permanent affair, but it used to be made of bamboo and was frequently washed away by the monsoon floods. But even though the bridge is modern, Sikkimese hospitality is the same as it ever was and the weary students are always welcomed into the small tea houses as well as the homes, where they are served not with tea but with a warm drink called *tomba*, a kind of millet beer. The fermented drink is served in a wide container and sucked up through a thin bamboo about a foot long. This strange but welcome drink helps to restore our students after the first day's trekking. Camp for that night is located away from the river because mountain rivers are usually unpredictable if there has been heavy rain in the mountains higher up and they swell unexpectedly in the night. No one wants to be caught by a sudden flood.

Leaving the tropical jungle of the Rangeet river in the early hours of the morning, the students now trek through forests accompanied by the chatter of monkeys and the calls of many kinds of birds; very beautiful are these tropical birds and the butterflies too, but in the wet season the forests are apt to be infested with leeches, which are not so pleasant. It is hot and the thick undergrowth hinders the movement of air; so the students long for the cool mountain breezes until eventually they leave the forest and its scent of wild orchids to enter the terraced fields where the Sikkimese farmers grow their millet, rice and corn. There are orange groves, too, and cardoman plantations. The houses are constructed of bamboo with thatched roofs and the people are always friendly and keep open house for the passing traveller. This was once true of Nepal too—and probably still is in some parts—but the increase in tourist trekking in the Nepalese mountains, with some of the trekkers accepting hospitality all along the way without thought of the cost to people who live anyway on the margin of existence, has resulted in a breakdown to some extent of the traditions of hospitality. No doubt, if the tourists begin to come to Sikkimin anything like the same numbers, the trouble will spread there too. But the old hospitality, which I first found on my earliest visit to Sikkim thirty years ago, is at present unchanged; this makes me very happy. You have to realise that the frontier of Sikkim had been closed for a time and has only just been reopened in a slightly restricted way, following some political upheaval. Tourism has never been developed there, but it will not be long now before it is seen in increasing proportions. For it is a very lovely country and those who can see it before it is spoilt will never forget it.

In the early hours of the afternoon, perhaps around two or three, the students begin to arrive at a hill top on which stands the small town of Penmayongtse. At its summit is one of Sikkim's oldest monasteries, small but very beautiful, with many ancient frescoes. I am told that the name Pemayongtse or Pemiongchi means, in fact, 'Monastery of the Sublime Lotus'. There are about twenty monks; the youngest is about six years old, while others are very aged and learned.

This first sight of the monastery is very welcome to the students, who often visit the building before even taking a rest. They make offerings and are blessed by the head lama. Even though most of our men are Hindus they have a great respect for Buddhism and do not hesitate to make offerings at any Buddhist monastery, for there are many more in this region besides the one at Pemayongtse, like those at Sanga Chelling and Tashiding, on the other side of the river. Tashiding means 'The Monastery of the Highest Bliss'.

On a clear day our base camp may be seen from Pemayongtse, but it is still a long way off, with great mountains towering around it and beyond: Kalim, Koktang, Kabru, Janu, Yogmuni, Narsing, Pandim, Simbhu and the great Kangchenjunga itself, most of them above 20,000 feet and the highest at 28,146 feet. The ridge from Kangchenjunga's summit southwards through Kabru and Koktang to Singalila forms the Nepalese frontier, and the British Kangchenjunga expedition of 1955 passed along the trough on the Nepalese side of the range.

Our camp is pitched upon a ridge near the monastery and very close to the old 'dak' bungalow where travellers may spend the night. The dak bungalows were originally built by the British authorities when long years ago Sikkim was open to them and they came up on horseback from the plains for their holidays. The trek the next day from Pemayongtse to Yoksam is notorious for leeches and the area is dreaded by students during the wet months when these creatures are voracious and liable to attack one seriously. We used to tell our men to cover their legs with a mixture of tobacco, salt and ash as a deterrent, but we later found that nylon socks reaching to the knees were much more effective.

This area is a mixture of forest and farmland. We descend to the cold, fast-flowing Ratong river, cross it by a bamboo bridge and then ascend to Yoksam. This little cluster of about twenty-five houses lies in a small valley, surrounded by high hills; its inhabitants are busy and contented people; their land is fertile, and cattle, poultry and pigs are plentiful. Yoksam means the 'Meeting Place of the Three Priests', for it was here that Thingong Salang is said to have welcomed the three lamas from Tibet, Pepchemchimbo, Kartoninzin and Ngagtap. Besides building all the great monasteries of Sikkim—Pemayongtse, Sanga Chelling, Dupti, Saigai, Tashiding, Talang and Thulong—legend says that the lamas decided that Sikkim needed a ruler and they did in fact choose its first ruler, whose name was Namgyal. The place where they met and took this decision is still pointed out in Yoksam.

Here at Yoksam we rest for another day so that the students may wash their clothes, enjoy local hospitality and continue their acclimatisation, for this is the last village through which they will pass before reaching base camp. When we leave it we climb up to Bakhim, at the height of 8,000 feet, where we pass through very dense forest in which deer, mountain goats and bears may be seen. These creatures roam the forests freely and are never hunted because the religion of the Sikkimese prohibits it. So the animals here are not afraid of man and do not regard him as an enemy. Sometimes leopards are seen and the very rare Himalayan panda; also musk deer. All these animals I have seen on a number of occasions. And the forest is filled with the scent of orchids.

Bakhim, which means 'land of bamboos' is just what its name suggests. The entire region of four miles by five is thick with bamboo, used for building in the villages around. We again cross a stream, the Prayg-cho, filled by the melting snows of the glaciers of Pandim rushing down through the Kangjob pass.

After another camp at Bakhim we climb steeply to Dzongri, from about 8,000 feet to over 13,000 feet, up through forests of silver fir, juniper, pine and rhododendron, azaleas, dwarf bamboo and Himalayan cherries. In May this part of the trek is especially beautiful, when all the rhododendrons, azaleas and primulas are in full flower and a blaze of colour. In fact the whole march from Darjeeling to base seems to pass through a garden, and when we reach Dzongri and have left the last trees behind—for we are then at last on the open mountain—it is as if the heavens themselves have opened up to reveal all the magnificent summits around us.

It is at Dzongri that the first signs of altitude sickness usually appear among our men, so we give them a rest for a day. But if many are affected badly by the height we send them down to Bakhim again for further acclimatisation. From Dzongri the base camp is only another 1,500 feet up.

Base camp is a camp of tents entirely; no huts. It is here that the real training begins, although by now most students will be fairly toughened up for the work ahead and during the previous fortnight, including the march, will have absorbed a great deal of theory and also done a little rockwork, besides learning how to accommodate themselves both to team-work and to high-altitude living.

Each day we go out from base in the morning at about seven or eight and come back in the afternoon about four, taking packed lunch with us just as if we were in the Alps of Switzerland. When we get back, if there has been rain or snow, there is time for relaxing, and for drying off clothing and equipment. Two weeks are passed here while the men are trained in all kinds of climbing, on rock and on ice, and are taken on actual climbs to give them graded practice in what they have been learning; and if a student has any special problem there is plenty of opportunity for him to discuss it and get help in putting it right before the course ends. Our training methods are exactly the same as those used by Dr Glatthard at Rosenlaui, with all the same apparatus. Of course, techniques change with the years, just a little all the time, and equipment has developed a lot since we began twenty years ago, but the essentials are the same and the Swiss Foundation has always kept us well informed about everything and has sent us new equipment for tryingout.

Our basic course will teach a man to become a reasonably competent mountaineer if he has any aptitude at all, and even if he has no later training he will be good enough at the end of the course to go out on any typical alpine-style climb without much difficulty. But not every student has the aptitude and some of them, it is soon clear, will not make the grade ever.

That fortnight's practical training, followed by the trek back to Darjeeling and a day or two for tidying up equip-ment, sorting out the marks and the cer-tificates and a closing ceremony completes the six-week course. No space has been given in this account to the great amount of detail covered by the course while in the mountains—everything from map-reading to the study of rock-for-mation, or from glacier rescue work to the climbing of fissures, chimneys, ledge traverses and so on, or how to handle emergencies of many kinds. There is a marking system, of course, with marks awarded for the several categories of work, with a silver badge for the best results and a bronze badge for those not quite so good, while those who fall below a certain level get nothing at all. If anyone should show really outstanding qualities, then he might get a special dis-tinction, but that would be rare.

Out of fifty students who take part we award, on the average, a full cer-tificate to perhaps five: that is to say we get a ten per cent result. To another twenty or so we say come back next year and try again; this group is not actually at all bad but have simply not achieved quite enough to deserve a certificate of real competence. The rest—about half the initial intake—are no good and in our estimation will never be any good; we do not encourage them to try again, since it would be a waste of time and money. Yet the result is not bad: five good climbers out of fifty, five whom we can send to the advanced course, is I think very worth while, for these are the men who, if they should pass their second course, as many of them do, will either become professional or at least end up as successful sport mountaineers. And among the middle category are some who, having come back for a second try, do pass in the end.

Most of those who get certificates at the end of the basic course do come back for the advanced course and end up with a full qualification. But it is not possible to go straight on from basic to advanced in the same year. Later some of the fully qualified people return to the Himalaya just for pleasure; others join expeditions with major objectives, while still others run expeditions of their own. There are many mountaineering clubs that organize quite serious expeditions to our mountains with their headquarters in the big cities and the universities. Some of the certificated men take up work in services that require mountain experience like surveying, but few in any case, even the least successful, go away without some benefit, physical or mental, from the weeks spent in the mountains with other men of like interests.

The advanced course is very different from the basic, and only men gaining certificates on the latter are admitted. The advanced course lasts two months and will turn the men out as highly qualified climbers, fit to compare with any in the world today. The base from which they work is farther up the same valley at a height of about 18,000 feet. It lies near a lake called Orne Chu at the foot of a whole group of glistening summits which provide these already fairly competent students with every possible kind of mountain problem. The view from the camp site is even more splendid than from the Kabur Saddle, but from the mountains slopes and summits themselves, especially from the face of Kabru Dome, immediately above the base, the great summits stand out bold and clear.

The climbs an advanced student takes are not limited to single-day expeditions; they take several days to complete, sometimes, and each party has to set up a proper chain of supplied camps, as on any major expedition, and afterwards dismantle them again and bring down the equipment. Every man has the chance to plan and organise a climb and to lead it. The instructors go with them -myself included—not to teach but to watch and correct—and to decide, on performance, the students' progress and final achievement. These mountains are all in the region of 20,000 feet; some are more and some are quite difficult, calling for all the student's strength and knowledge and intelligence. To succeed is a high performance by any standard. There is no third course; once we had a pre-Everest course, but that was something special.

So far there have been no serious accidents to either students or instructors. For a twenty-year history I think that is a great record. All our troubles have been medical ones, simple illness, almost always pulmonary, the result of the altitude and poor acclimatisation. Remember that some of these men have never been on a mountain before, certainly nothing like a Himalayan mountain. The trouble usually starts with coughing, which is quickly noticed by instructors or doctor. Anyone heard coughing is carefully watched from that moment on. If the cough gets worse or does not soon clear up, we take rapid action, especially when the cough has started at 15,000 feet or thereabouts, as it usually does. We send the patient down at once to much lower levels. It takes a day and a night to get him down to 5,000 feet, where he will be safe and make a quick recovery. There is nothing else to be done; there are no effective medicines for this sort of trouble and no doctor can do more than we do. It is not serious so long as action is taken at once; in the valley the man gets better quite quickly, but he must never again be allowed to go up to high altitudes, because his lungs are simply not suited to them. It is best for his own sake that he should keep away. Otherwise it is absolutely certain that the cough will come back and it could easily become fatal.

It is interesting that in my experience younger people are not so good at really high altitudes as are older men. Many mountaineers of about forty years of age, even older, have the right strength and physique and mind for serious expeditionary work. And if they keep themselves fit and in training they can go on for years more. It is not necessarily a question of breathing trouble, though that is a factor; it is something in the head. Lots of otherwise fit young climbers have giddiness and a lot of vomiting; but this seems to pass with years. In fact, at the start of their careers a lot of young Sherpas suffer from mountain sickness, which may seem surprising having regard to their origins. Eventually, in most cases, it passes away as they gain in experience, confidence and acclimatisation. Acclimatisation is something that seems to stay with you; even if you come back to the high altitudes after quite a long interval, it is not difficult to get back again to the right adjustment, at least not so difficult as it was on previous occasions. I have heard that quite a lot of European climbers admit to a certain amount of mountain sickness at the beginning of their careers and especially when they come out from European altitudes to Himalayan altitudes. I have no experience of this. My lungs were made in the Himalaya, like my legs and my heart, and they are not troubled. In my view you can be too young for climbing Everest or any other very high mountain; the best age is between twenty-eight and forty years. Mountains give little trouble to older men once they are used to them.

It will be seen from this account of student training at HMI that, although I have not taken part in any expedition since 1953, I still spend a great deal of time in climbing at very high altitudes, probably more than most enthusiastic mountaineers. I always accompany the students into Sikkim unless I happen to be travelling abroad—and this means that I go on foot five times a year from Darjeeling to the mountain base camps, and from there to the highest points in their training, probably at 21,000 feet or even more. I lecture to them on expedition planning and organisation during the eight-day approach march; I climb with them on snow and ice and rock; I go with them from camp to camp to very great heights; I live with them all the time and I share their life entirely. So in every single year I cover a lot of ground and a lot of height, and this does not leave me with much time for any other climbing activity. But because I am with them all the time I can properly assess each student's true ability, and in good time I am able to recommend them—or not—to various expeditions as men of proper experience, if I am asked to do so. I still get a lot of satisfaction out of this sort of mountaineering and to it is added the special pleasure of training others to climb their Everests, as I once did myself.

6: ACHIEVEMENT

I have said that any student who successfully completes our advanced course has reached a very high standard of mountaineering ability. In fact a remarkable number of our students have gone on to participate in a number of major expeditions and have shown how well they can do.

The first of these took place only a year after our opening, in 1955, when 'Nandu' Jayal, our Principal, led an expedition to Kamet in North Gharwal. This mountain is 25,447 feet high and is a most striking one to look upon. It seems to stand high above all the surrounding summits, a magnificent pyramid, and thousands of feet above the glaciers to east and west. The view for those who get to the summit is said to be very grand indeed, stretching far out over the ranges into the distant purple plain of Tibet.

When Major Jayal took his expedition there in 1955 it had been climbed only once, in 1931 by Frank Smythe, an English climber with whom I worked on two later expeditions to Everest, 1935 and 1938. Smythe was a frequent visitor to the Himalaya, either to climb or to search for mountain flowers, and I last saw him only a short while befcre his death in 1949 when he was in Darjeeling preparing for a trip with me into the hills to photograph and collect plants. Already the disease that killed him was apparent in his speech and manner. He was an extremely likeable man and when he died I felt that I had lost a very close friend indeed. Jayal's expedition to Kamet to attempt its second conquest was the first expedition in which the Institute was directly involved. It was to give proof of the hard work we had done in our first year. It gave a great sense of achievement to mountaineering in India, because it was highly successful in the outcome.

On this expedition there were two of our advanced students: Captain J. D. Dias and Captain R. K. Malhotra, and five of our Sherpa instructors, besides Major Jayal himself. There were also two men from the Bengal sappers, a regiment that had already tried this mountain twice before, in 1952 and 1953, and had been very nearly successful on both attempts. Four of the five Sherpas were among those who went with me to Dr Glatthard's school at Rosenlaui: Ang Tharkay, Gyalzen Mikchen, Da Namgyal and Ang Tempa. One of the aims of the trip was to give practice to the instructor staff of the Institute and also a change from their routines. In fact it was a sort of combined expedition and training exercise.

The climb was successful at a second attempt and three of our instructors were in the summit party. The first attempt, too, had been very nearly successful, but dusk settled upon the summit party only about sixty feet below the summit (in the vertical sense) and a hundred and fifty feet away from it (in distance). Had they gone on, darkness and the great cold might have had serious consequences for them all. But the second try did come off and for us at HMI this was a great beginning. Major Jayal has described the view as 'absolutely magnificent' and I can well believe it, for the weather was good and the sky clear and they could see far and wide over rock and ice summits, with Mana and Nanda Devi quite close and Chaukamba more distant but huge. It was, incidentally, the first time that four Sherpas of an expedition had climbed a high peak. Also, on the way up two flowering plants were discovered on a ridge at over 20,000 feet high which are thought to be the highest growing plants ever found; they were taken back to the Forest Research Institute.

On this expedition there were no mishaps to mar its success. While Jayal and his group were ascending Kamet, Captain Dias with Gurdial Singh of Doon School went off to attempt Abi Gamin and were seen by the successful Kamet party arriving at its summit. A double success.

An Indian attempt on Everest was made in 1960, led by Brigadier Gyan Singh of the Indian Army who later became Principal of HMI. In the meantime an Indian team had successfully climbed Cho Oyu, the eighth highest mountain in the world, and Indian mountaineers were encouraged to make an attempt on the highest of all. In India the sport was growing fast. To prepare for this new venture the Institute organised a special pre-Everest course quite close to our training area in Sikkim in the autumn of 1959. Twenty-five climbers were tried out and the final team for 1960 was based upon the recommendations of Brigadier Gyan Singh and myself. In fact there turned out to be more competent climbers than places for them in the team, but we finally selected thirteen.

There was also the question of equipment and we thought it would be a good thing if as much as possible could be manufactured in India. For the most part the Indian material turned out perfectly and this was a particularly rewarding aspect of the venture. Under my supervision, moreover, Sherpa and Nepali women worked very hard to knit woollen wear for the climbers, and the Swiss Foundation gave a great deal of technical assistance.

I took no part in the actual expedition, only in its preparation and in the selection of the team, so I cannot describe it from personal experience. It was my job to organise the Sherpas and the porters; at Jaynagar railhead there were over 700 of them to register, to divide the loads among and to split into appropriate groups, since so huge a column could scarcely march off all at once.

My nephew Gombu, who was in the Everest expedition of 1953 and is today my deputy at HMI, took part in the expedition and so did Sonam, a great Indian mountaineer about whom I will tell later. Though the expedition failed to get to the top, its achievement was great. The route taken was the one used by previous parties, through the Khumbu ice-fall and the Western Cwm, across the Lhotse Face to South Col and finally up the South Ridge. The problems were therefore largely known, though in fact the mountains are constantly changing and are never the same from one year to another. And of nothing is this more true than the Khumbu ice-fall, which changes with every day; men and equipment and stores have to move through it all the time an expedition is on the mountain if the upper camps and climbers are to be kept properly supplied. Yet the great masses of ice are breaking up continually and new giant crevasses opening and bridges, so carefully placed, disappearing. At least one recent expedition has avoided the difficulties by using a helicopter to dump supplies beyond the fall; a sign of the times which, if developed, will make some of the biggest mountains almost too simple.

Eventually the last camp was set up at about 1,500 feet below the summit. Kumar was there with Sonam and Gombu, but in the night the wind became very strong and in the morning, when the climbers set out for the top, a real gale was raging. That Everest wind! Don't I know it! Terrible! It defeated Lambert and me in 1952; the terrifying strength of it, the noise, the constant battering and tearing, the exhaustion of even trying to stand up, the snow that is flung into your face and goggles and can block up the valves of your oxygen system, and the great cold that numbs your thinking as well as your body. But the three Indians set off nevertheless, after waiting hopefully for the wind to drop a little; it did not drop and there was no more time to waste.

Keeping below the crest of the ridge to avoid the full blast, they made steady progress until at last forced to expose themselves by taking to the ridge. The wind increased. They could scarcely see or breathe. At noon they halted about 700 feet below the summit and, although the temptation to go on was great, they realised that the possibility of reaching the top and getting back again was small. They decided to give up. The next day the monsoon fell on the range thoroughly and, after a brief wait in the hope of a temporary break, the whole expedition was withdrawn, for a further effort could have been to risk disaster. In the mountains it is a good thing to know when to turn back.

Nevertheless, the first Indian attempt on Everest was a big achievement and the expedition had a lot of reason to be proud of itself. It showed how far Indian mountaineering had progressed in a very short time and the Institute could congratulate itself on its direct contribution. Our young men had shown themselves fully fit to tackle the world's highest mountain; we had made a lot of our own material and it had stood up to the severe test; we had solved our own organisational problems very effectively. Lastly, there had been no casualties. This climb was a great stimulus to Indian mountaineering and in the following year many wholly Indian expeditions went up into the Himalaya and many peaks were climbed, with former students of HMI as well as Sherpas taking part.

The greatest and most exciting of all Indian expeditions came five years later with the all- Indian Everest expedition of 1965, when no fewer than nine climbers reached the top; eight of them were former students of HMI and some actually had begun their careers as basic course men; they had then gone on to the advanced course and when it was again necessary to choose men for Everest, they had gone on a pre-Everest course. The ninth successful climber was Nepalese. My nephew was one of the first pair to reach the summit, but by this time he had already been there once, having climbed it with James Whitaker of the American 1963 expedition. I had given Gombu a statue of the Buddha to leave up there in the snow, and this he did. So although I am myself one of the first two men ever to reach the highest point on earth, I have a nephew who has been there twice, the only man to achieve this distinction. On the second occasion he spent the night at the highest camp ever pitched on the mountain at 27,930 feet.

The terrible Everest wind again played its evil part in the story, delaying the start for several days. Even at base camp it could be heard whistling and shrieking its way across the ridges, sweeping clouds of snow before it, while the tents, big and small, shook and trembled like leaves. But at last the wind dropped and the morning of 16 May dawned clear. Gombu and his companion Cheema moved up from advanced base to Camp IV and on the 18th reached South Col. The next morning was again clear and bright; the two climbers set out early and the going was good. Nearer and nearer they drew to the South Summit until at last they were on the hump immediately below it. Here their ten supporters pitched the two-man tent at almost 28,000 feet, with little more than a thousand feet to go. The morning was cloudy and the wind was stronger, but the two climbers were in good condition and, having slept well, were at the South Summit by eight o'clock. An hour and a half later the Indian flag was at the top of the world, where the flag and pole left by James Whitaker and Gombu two years earlier still stood.

That was 20 May. Another party reached the summit two days later but they were less lucky with the weather; the wind was fierce and the snow was soft and deep. They lost their way once; Ang Dawa suffered frost-bite; Sonam was in pain; Da Norbu was very exhausted. But they got there. On the 24th, a glorious day for weather, Vohra and Kami, too, succeeded in a fine and uneventful climb; only on the descent did they have trouble. And on the 29th the fourth and last group reached the summit. The whole expedition was off the mountain two days later. It had been an extraordinary performance, done, as the leader later wrote, on the shoulders of the predecessors, but a great tribute to the skill and strength of Indian mountaineering. How far we had come!

Pandit Nehru had asked me to train a thousand Tenzings. I cannot claim to have personally trained all the men concerned in these great climbs, though eight of the nine summit men had in fact passed through the Institute. It was a triumph for the Institute as well as for the individual climbers. Yet the curious fact is that when the 1965 expedition returned to India many receptions were arranged to celebrate their achievement but not a single invitation was sent to me to take part in them. Later they came to Darjeeling and were given a warm reception by the Sherpa Climbers' Association and the people of Darjeeling; on this occasion I did my duty. Similarly, although I had no real wish to climb Everest a second or third time, nevertheless when three separate Indian expeditions were arranged to climb Everest, I was never invited to take part, for the simple reason, I am firmly convinced, that Indian climbers did not want me on their expeditions despite all that I have done for Indian mountaineering and the twenty years I have spent on training their climbers.

During the year previous to the Everest triumph, 1964, an Indian team had gone to Nanda Devi (25,645 feet), the highest point in the central Himalaya, a very beautiful mountain. You can see it from Ranikhet, a sort of centrepiece in the whole range of snow peaks forming the horizon. The approach is quite difficult and leads through one of the greatest river gorges in the world, where the Rishiganga flows.

The base of this mountain was not reached until the 1930s and the mountain itself was not conquered until H. W. Tilman and N. E. Odell got there in 1936. The eastern summit was reached by a Polish party three years later and that was the summit I climbed with a French party in 1951: it was the hardest climb I have ever done, before or since, Everest included. I did it with Dubost and we were only the second party ever to have got there. But all real pleasure in the ascent was clouded by the fact that we were all the time searching for traces of two Frenchmen who had gone up the main summit earlier and had not returned. When at last Dubost and I stood on top of Nanda Devi East, after a long, terribly steep and dangerous ridge climb, over humps and needles sheeted with ice and new snow, always in danger of a fall, we searched with our eyes the whole ridge to the main summit and saw not the slightest sign of Duplat and Vignes, nor any evidence of their having ever passed that way. It is a terrible ridge, about two miles long, very narrow and falling steeply on either side, a sort of thin white ribbon, rising and falling and twisting, with empty blueness to right and left. I think that the two missing men must have tried to traverse it from the one summit to the other and fallen somewhere on the way. Anyway they were never seen again.

Major Jayal had been on that French expedition of 1951, too, and he had gone back there in 1957 with the first all-Indian expedition to the mountain; but the weather had been against them that year and they were forced to give up when only 500 feet from the summit. There was another unsuccessful Indian attempt in 1961, and yet another in 1964 under Major Kumar, and this was a success at last. Gombu, my nephew, was one of the summit pair, Dawa Norbu being the other man. Originally there had been three on the rope but V. P. Vohra, who was one of the nine who got to the top of Everest later, had to stop when only a few hundred feet from success.

Quite recently—in the spring of 1975 to be exact—Nanda Devi has been climbed again, this time by an Indo-French expedition. Both summits were reached, the east peak as well as the main peak, and the climbers had intended to make the traverse from one to the other. But although the ridge was closely examined from both ends and some of it explored, the traverse was never actually completed. So this extraordinarily beautiful and extremely difficult ridge remains virgin—a shining, twisting white ribbon high in the thin blue air, a scene such as I have never seen since—or before—in all my mountain experience.

Most of the Indian climbers on this expedition were military men and all had been trained by HMI. One of them, Aloka Chandola, was a nephew of Nandu Jayal, my one-time chief who had taken part in the Nanda Devi expedition of twenty years earlier. Among them, too, was Dorje Lhatoo, who is married to my niece Doma; his father was Tibetan and his mother came from Namche Bazar. He was one of our instructors in Darjeeling. Amongst the Sherpas in the team was my old friend Gyaltzen, who served as the expedition's cook and had been an HMI instructor too.

After this expedition the French climbers spoke in ecstatic terms of the beautiful approach march to the mountain, a march I too remember vividly from long ago: the flowers in the forests, the gentians and other mountain plants, the magnolias and giant rhododendrons, the many beautifully coloured birds and the innumerable butterflies. In their account of the climb the French have described it as the 'impossible ascent'; it is not 'impossible', of course, and there is no such thing anywhere. Very difficult, yes, but one day the traverse will be done and probably soon; what makes it especially hazardous is the exhausting and quite difficult ascent you have to make before you start out on a couple of miles of exceedingly airy mountaineering. The French climbers suffered rather a lot of casualties: one climber had a heart attack, another suffered partial paralysis, another had severe pneumonia, and others suffered fractures or bruises from falls and avalanches. They were not very lucky.

One of the first batch of students selected by me for training in the year that the Institute opened its doors was Sonam Gyatso, who soon became one of India's greatest mountaineers. In 1957 he was in Major Jayal's unsuccessful Nanda Devi expedition, but in 1958 he reached the top of Cho Oyu with Sherpa Pasang Dawa Lama, only the second time that Cho Oyu, the eighth highest mountain in the world, had been climbed. And on the first Indian expedition to Everest he was one of the outstanding climbers, getting to within 700 feet of the summit with two others in a raging blizzard. In 1961 he was with an Indian expedition to Annapurna III and with M. S. Kohli successfully climbed the highest virgin peak reached till then by an all-Indian party.

On that Annapurna expedition there was trouble with the inhabitants of the region, and Sonam and one of his companions were taken hostage and held to ransom. Sonam carried through the negotiations that followed with great tact and skill. In the autumn of the same year he successfully climbed another virgin peak, Kangshenjau (21,602 feet) and in 1962 was again on Everest, this time being forced to withdraw only 400 feet from the top, again by raging blizzards. But in 1965 he did reach the summit and spent an hour there; he was then forty-two years old and it was his third attempt. It had been a wonderful climb, for the wind was blowing at sixty miles an hour and it seemed quite impossible that anyone should ever succeed in such conditions. Sonam's back was frostbitten and he passed the night before the ascent in great pain. He went on because he did not want to fail again. And he did not fail. Sonam died three years later of an incurable disease and India lost one of her greatest climbers, one of whom the Institute was very proud indeed.

I have told these stories—there are so many more, of course, but I have not room for all—to show just what Indian mountaineering has achieved in the years since the ascent of Everest in 1953 and quite a lot as a result of the labours of HMI. Today there are many expeditions every season in which our former pupils and our instructors take part, not always to big and famous mountains, because they take a long time to organise and cost a lot of money to carry out; but height and fame are not everything. As in Europe climbers in India are becoming more interested in technical problems than in collecting or repeating famous summits, and for that matter some of the lower summits provide difficulties quite as serious as their bigger neighbours. The business of rushing out for the famous mountains—Everest, Kangchenjunga, K2—is largely over, but there are still lots of things to do in the Himalaya and mountains to climb for the first time, and Indians are doing them.

We train now three Sherpas every year at HMI; at first it was six, but the number was reduced because it is difficult for so many trained men to find the work to suit them afterwards. These three Sherpas get the fullest training, right through the advanced course, and it costs them nothing; the whole thing is a gift from the Indian Government. With this behind them they are usually able to find enough work, mainly as high altitude porters on foreign expeditions that come to climb mostly in Nepal. When the Americans took an expedition to Dhaulagiri in 1973, two of these Sherpas got to the top of the mountain. Later I met one of the American climbers in New York and he told me how well trained he found the Sherpas to be: 'We did not have to teach them a thing,' he said. 'They taught us and they often led the climb. ' Our Sherpa students all come from Solu Khumbu and when they complete the course they get our certificate and badge, just as mountain guides do in Europe.

However, the number of expeditions requiring fully trained Sherpas is not all that great, and tourism and trekking are scarcely the right work for certificated climbers. So some of our fully trained Sherpas pass on to other schools of mountaineering in India—there are many now—to take up work as instructors in their turn, while a few join those services that require men with mountain knowledge and skill. The other climbing schools in India do not run advanced courses like ours in Darjeeling; nevertheless our former Sherpa students are passing on, during the basic course, the methods and techniques they learnt at HMI.

Until 1973 the Institute had conducted a total of eighty-five basic courses and fifty-six advanced courses, and every year it provides in addition a special course for women, which has been most successful, with just as many students as the men's basic course. I find that the women students take the instruction more seriously than the men do. Daku, my wife, has passed the advanced course and has climbed as high as 21,000 feet in our training area. During my term of office as Director of Field Training since 1954, 4,628 students have been trained on our mountaineering courses: 3,020 basic students, 492 advanced students, and 1,116 students on adventure courses. Seven of these trainees climbed to the top of Everest in 1965.

All the instructors are fully employed throughout the year, except for their official holidays; when there are no climbing duties for them at Darjeeling they go to other parts of India—to Calcutta or Mysore or Bombay, for instance—to teach rock-climbing. There are eleven instructors altogether, and four of them are still from the group of six which in 1954 trained with me in Switzerland: Gyaltzen Mikcha, Da Namgyal, Ang Tempa and Gombu. Ang Tharkay has stopped climbing and is now a successful business man in Darjeeling. Ang Nyima, who was one of those Sherpas who climbed highest on the 1953 Everest expedition, for a time was in the British Army, but has now retired to become a farmer in Darjeeling, keeping cows and pigs and chickens, and has built himself a three-storey house. I wish he were still with us. Others will be retiring soon. Our instructors, old or young alike, are all Sherpas and are among the best professional climbers in the world. They are all well educated and speak many languages—Sherpa, Tibetan, Sikkimese, English, Hindi, Nepali, Bengali—all these and others too. And we are proud of them: they are honest, strong, competent—the best you could find anywhere.

Their living conditions are quite comfortable. The starting salary is about Rs. 200 per month, rising in time to Rs. 700, but there is a daily allowance and other benefits. They all get their food free and a house free too, for themselves and their families. Each house has two bedrooms, a bathroom, a dining-room and a kitchen, as well as a garden. And on retirement they can look forward to a pension.

The Institute long ago took over the job of supplying expeditions with Sherpas, which was previously done by the Himalayan Club. In the old days the men were not trained as they are now and the wages were low. The Club fixed all the charges. In 1963 we founded a Sherpa Climbers Association, both to help the expeditions and to look after the Sherpas' interests. Membership is strictly for certificated climbers of Sherpa origin, those who have been through the Institute's courses or have taken part in major expeditions already and have shown the proper skill. This really does make sure of proper standards which expeditions can rely on and it maintains the reputation of our people. This organisation is what Pandit Nehru recommended and the Association has government approval.

Before 1953, if a Sherpa was killed on an expedition the compensation amounted to only Rs. 500 (about £30) for a married man and half that sum for a single man. Not much. Maybe if you lost your donkey you might get more! Now we have a fixed compensation of Rs. 3,000 for a married man and Rs. 2,000 for a single man. Now we are trying to arrange for every man to be insured by the expedition he joins for Rs. 10,000. Their daily wage is fixed at Rs. 6, plus food and an equipment allowance, all very much better than in the old days when I first went climbing, but it still needs improving. I am President of the Association and Pem-Pem is its Secretary.

I have spoken of the much-improved conditions for which our instructors and other Sherpas work. I ought to say that for a number of reasons, some of which I simply do not understand, these improvements do not seem to have come to me. But I will discuss this elsewhere.

7: PEM-PEM AND NIMA GO CLIMBING

Although the Institute officially opened in the autumn of 1954, at the start in fact the number of students was quite small and I was occupied largely with preparational work for the years when the intake would be much larger. This left me free when December came, with fine weather in the Himalaya and good conditions in the foothills, to take my two daughters, Pem-Pem and Nima, on the long trek from the Indian plain through Dharan to Namche Bazar, the chief place in Solu Khumbu. Their cousin Doma came too. Doma is my elder sister's daughter who, some years after the events recorded in this chapter, married Dorje Lahtoo, one of my instructors at HMI; she now has three sons, all at the Mount Hermon School.

My daughters had been born in Darjeeling and had never before visited my native valley, nor had they ever seen their grandmother, who was still living at Namche Bazar but had never been to Darjeeling. I thought it was about time they all met and that my daughters should meet the people of the region, including their relatives, and get to know something of real Sherpa ways. At the time of the trek Pem-Pem was not yet sixteen years old and her sister was a year younger.

We left Darjeeling on Christmas Day. We travelled by motor from the railway to Dharan, a small town on the Nepalese frontier, on the edge of the thickly forested Terai, and then took the traditional route northwards, rapidly ascending into the hills and forests of southern Nepal, descending sharply to cross many rivers and rising again to the crests beyond. About half-way the route is joined by the one from Kathmandu, coming in from the west. It took us sixteen days to cover the journey, which is average time; it was all done on foot. Like myself, the girls carried all their possessions on their backs, making their way to Namche in the way the Sherpas have done for centuries. It was something they had never experienced before and they enjoyed it very much; it is a fairly strenuous journey on what in those days was a fairly rough trail, but they proved to be true Sherpas, strong and tireless, taking to mountain travel as naturally as a duck to water. We stayed in the villages on the trail and the people there went out of their way to entertain us, for these were the days when both mountains and people were still unspoilt and the tourist business had damaged neither. When we got to Namche every house was opened to us and there was a huge welcome, with drinking and dancing and much feasting. A Sherpa rejoicing is something to see.

From Namche we continued the trek to Thami, the village where I spent much of my boyhood and from which I went up to look after the yaks on the high pastures while I gazed at the mountain summits and dreamed of the day when I would reach the tops myself. We also followed the Everest trail from Namche, through Khumjung as far as Thyangboche and Dingboche, but on this trip we stopped short before reaching glacier level and did not reach the site of the original base camp. Nevertheless, Nima and Pem-Pem got their first close view of Everest, the mountain that made the Sherpas famous throughout the world, the mountain on whose topmost snows I had trod only a little while before. In shining weather the great summits filled the sky, Everest itself unmistakable, brilliant and huge, and all around the giant circle of supporters. Breathtakingly beautiful.

In all the villages of the upper Khumbu we were given the same warm welcome as at Namche, the same hospitality, for this was only a year and a half since the great climb and the memory of it was still as strong among the Sherpas as if it were yesterday. The flood of visitors from the outside world was yet a long way off, and the people of Khumbu, by nature happy and hospitable, were overjoyed to see us.

At the end of the trip we took my mother back with us to Darjeeling, which of course included the long switchback trek to Dharan at eighty-four years of age, which she managed very well. She had never seen the world outside the valley and she found many surprises, some of which gave us much amusement, especially when she described a train as 'a whole house moving'. From then on she lived with us in Darjeeling and died there some years later.

The trek to Namche was repeated the next year, 1955, when we left Darjeeling on 17 December and this time pushed our journey as far as the original base camp site and also to Camp 1. Many western people make this journey today by one of several routes and the trails have changed a great deal as a result. The route from Jaynagar in the Indian plain was always a traditional trade one for mule caravans and pedestrians northwards into Tibet, very busy in the summer months with the carriage of rice and sugar and paper especially, and on the southward journey of salt and wool for India. Political events have, of course, diminished the traffic. At first it leads through fairly prosperous farming country, and later over many ridges, constantly up and down, through great mossy forests of huge but—in the right season—vividly-coloured rhododendrons, across immense gorges with precarious bamboo suspension bridges over the roaring torrents, bridges which today are giving way to more modern structures. Occasionally there are glimpses, beyond the blue-green hills, of the high Himalaya in white array along the skyline to the north, but never Everest, which remains hidden throughout the journey until you are well beyond Namche. But when at last you get into the valley of the Dudh Kosi, where the river runs like a twisting silver thread through its narrow gorge, the land is grand and wild indeed.

Unchanged till about a dozen years ago, this trail is now followed by many organised groups of tourists, accompanied by Sherpa guides and porters, complete with tents, kitchen equipment and even special lavatory tents. The organised parties bring their own food for the most part, but even these reckon to buy some things—like chickens and eggs—on the road; the independent groups, however, very often reckon to live off the land entirely, carrying as little as possible, unguided and with practically no equipment. This is very thoughtless.

All of them, organised or not, tramp up the valleys and over the ridges on the once primitive trail that leads to Namche Bazar and the scene of the struggle in the early 'fifties for the summit of Everest. Their passing has left its mark on the land. Many leave their rubbish by the roadside and cut the forests down for fuel. The Sherpa guides do their cooking on wood fires and like to have a good big fire after dark, for it can be cold in the mountains; so you have only to think about how much wood must be used for the fires of a single party of a dozen tourists with about thirty or more guides and porters, three times a day. Then multiply that many times for all the parties in a season and you can realise the dreadful destruction of the forests. The trees that are being destroyed are not being replaced. Things can only get worse with the years if nothing is done to stop it. The tourists who come to Nepal to see the wilderness are actually destroying it as they go along.

Huts for refreshment—beer, tea, chang—have sprung up along the way. There is an airstrip at Lukla for light airplanes which arrive from Kathmandu several times a day, and there is a Japanese-built hotel with oxygen available for guests who fall sick from the effects of the high altitude. Now they have made another airstrip farther up the valley, even closer to Everest, at Shyangboche. Food wrappings, beer cans, untidy campsites, toilet paper, rubbish and the remains of fires, are becoming more common to see with every year that passes. Hippies have been seen for some years past in the region of Thyangboche monastery.

So the tourists and hippies who first reached the Solu Khumbu valley only a few years ago are already responsible for a great deal of pollution and destruction, as well as for a big change in the Sherpa way of life. Children have been known to demand 'baksheesh' quite angrily from passing trekkers, a thing unheard of in the past; monks and nuns, too, ask for alms along the road; itinerant Tibetans offer cheap trinkets and jewellery for sale. Some of the trekkers, especially Americans, thoughtlessly give large tips to Sherpa guides and porters, which the men—who can blame them?—soon learn to accept as normal, even if the sum is more than they would have earned in a whole year not long ago. Some attempts have been made to discourage this, but it is already too late. It all makes for a very different atmosphere from that of the near past and I think it makes some of the older Sherpas very sad. The tourists rush around taking photographs of everything everywhere, sometimes asking for permission, often not, and some of the Sherpas have got around now to asking fees for a pose. Many of the younger people welcome such changes, of course, with the employment it brings in and the money, put these are the people who themselves move out of the valley sooner or later, attracted by the idea of an easier life elsewhere, which does not always follow.

In 1954 and 1955 none of this had taken place. It did not really develop until the later 'sixties and even then on a small scale only. Now it is increasing every year. So when my daughters travelled with me the route to Namche Bazar, conditions were not a lot different from what they had been for many generations and the Sherpa people were not much affected by contact with the West—a little, of course, by the expeditions that had passed through, but the old ways were still more or less intact. The girls saw Solu Khumbu as it was when the British expedition was there and they enjoyed it greatly.

On the second trip I took them up to see the Khumbu ice-fall before the retreat of the glacier which has so changed the scene during the last twenty years, reducing the upper valley to a huge accumulation of boulders and rotting ice where once there had been a great stretch of glacier, crevasses and a maze of pinnacle ice.

It was not surprising therefore that both Pem-Pem and Nima, and Doma too, responded eagerly to an invitation to join a proper expedition when it came five years later. They were full of enthusiasm about the idea of climbing to really high places.

It was in July 1959 that an expedition made up entirely of women left Europe for Nepal; it was the first of its kind ever to be seen in the Himalaya. It was international and its leader was Claude Kogan, a French lady with very great experience in climbing in the Alps, Andes and Himalaya. She was quite a small person, very good-looking but strong, and her achievements were quite famous amongst climbing people. She had already climbed Nun Kun in Kashmir (23,410 feet) in 1953 as one of a small party in which Major Jayal was included. This had been a virgin peak. She had done a lot besides that. Now her objective was Cho Oyu at nearly 27,000 feet on the Tibetan frontier not far west of Everest. You can see it from Everest in fact. But I have never been there myself. To reach it you follow the Everest route as far as Namche Bazar, then you turn westwards for the Nangpa La, a pass of about 19,000 feet on the frontier about three or four days' march away. From this pass you really see Cho Oyu for the first time as well as the vast and purple plains of Tibet to the north. Base camp for Cho Oyu is not very far from the pass.

Madame Kogan had already made an attempt on Cho Oyu about five years earlier in the company of my good friend Raymond Lambert, with whom I had climbed on Everest, but their attempt had failed when the weather changed abruptly on the very day after the mountain had been ascended for the first time by the Austrian climber Herbert Tichy with another Austrian and the Sherpa

Pasang Dawa Lama. Raymond and Madame Kogan were less than 2,000 feet from the top when they were forced to give up by a sudden fall in the temperature and by fierce winds. The winter storms had come and for Cho Oyu it was already too late.

The sad fact of that failure was that Raymond and Madame Kogan could have reached the summit safely in the first place, but they had agreed to stand aside to allow Tichy to make his attempt, his second attempt, on the mountain. For Tichy had arrived at the mountain first, unaware that Lambert was also on his way there, and had in fact already made one attempt but had been forced down by terrifying winds and had suffered severe frostbite to his hands. Anyway, Tichy got there first and succeeded at the second attempt, and then the weather finally closed in and drove everyone down. Tichy's Sherpa—Pasang Dawa Lama—who had gone down to Namche to get supplies, achieved the astonishing feat of tramping up from the village of Marlung and climbing to the summit of Cho Oyu in three days. Afterwards Raymond was criticised for ever starting up the mountain while another party was there already climbing, but I cannot feel that the criticism is justified. After all, he and Claude Kogan did wait for the result of Tichy's attempt and did not interfere in any way; Tichy and Lambert had in any case agreed between them who was to go first. And it was Raymond who welcomed Tichy back and congratulated him warmly. Tichy himself never complained.

It seems that climbing Cho Oyu is rather a matter of timing. But that is not unusual. The same can well be said of Everest and many other Himalayan summits. Eric Shipton had made an attempt on Cho Oyu in 1952 before the monsoon and had been stopped by an ice barrier which he thought might take two weeks to pass. It was he who told Tichy that the period after the monsoon might be better. So Tichy set out from Kathmandu at the beginning of September and reached the summit on 19 October. On the first attempt Tichy and Pasang feared for their lives in the cruel gale that swept the unprotected slopes of snow. In trying to save the Sherpas' tent from blowing away, Tichy accidentally plunged his hands into the snow; they went numb and white. Then the whole party raced off the mountain in order to save them and to escape a wind that could kill them all if they waited. That was when Lambert turned up.

When Madame Kogan came back to Cho Oyu in 1959 she had decided to be on the mountain three weeks earlier, to get the better weather, which meant leaving Kathmandu in August. Perhaps a little early, I thought; a little later might be better, since after the monsoon there can be too much soft snow around, very tiring to climb through, also very dangerous and liable to avalanche if the weather gets warm. It needs a little time to settle and leave a fine firm surface for crampons. After that there may be a few days of fine weather when the mountain may be climbed, but the good weather period is quite short and difficult to forecast. It changes quickly.

With Madame Kogan were her English deputy, Countess Gravina, two other English ladies, three Frenchwomen, one Swiss and one Belgian, and of course the Sherpas. Wangdi was sirdar and my nephew Gombu was there too. Then it was suggested to me, why should my two daughters and also my niece not join the expedition? Not one of them had ever before done any serious climbing, though they were all really strong girls and fit for the task. Yet trekking to Namche, even though it was then a very different thing from what it is today, is not exactly a climb or adequate training for a proper climb. The proposition in fact looked a little foolhardy, both for the expedition and for the girls. Many friends advised against it, and I was very uneasy. In the end I let them go. Furthermore, they had to get permission to stay away from school for all those weeks.

I was in Kathmandu when the ladies arrived from Europe, for they had given me the job of making all the necessary arrangements there, especially the organisation of porters and their loads. The three girls were already with me, waiting to start. So on 21 August I saw the whole caravan off on the long trek: twelve ladies and their baggage.

None of the European ladies had ever been to Namche before – except their leader—but of course my daughters now knew the area well and on the way were able to tell their companions a great deal about it. The party halted at Namche for four days because the weather was poor and the monsoon was still at work on the mountains. Eventually they reached the Nangpa La on 14 September and straight away set about establishing their chain of camps. It was the leader's decision that the women should do everything—or almost every-thing—themselves, with only minor help from the Sherpas. For this was a women's expedition.

It ended in tragedy. The weather was poor from the start, with storms and lots of heavy new snow. A great deal of time was spent in making good the damage and dis-organisation caused by the snowstorms, and load-carrying became very tiring. Sometimes it even became uncomfortably warm; a few hours later it would be snowing again, and the snow was soft and unstable. And there was sickness too. Even in the lower camps some of the women suffered from the altitude. Pem-Pem herself had a bad headache, which is not unusual when getting used to higher altitudes, and one of the climbers had to retreat to Namche Bazar for much the same reason. Another lady broke a blood vessel and she, too, had to retreat. The expedition's doctor had to go down with them, as well as some of the porters, and this reduced the available manpower, and womanpower too, of course.

At the end of the month the chain of camps was estab-lished. The weather seemed better. Too warm perhaps during the day and the snow too soft, so that people slid about a lot and got rather exhausted. Then suddenly the weather broke up. Madame Kogan and Claudine Van der Stratten, the Belgian lady, were up at Camp III and making ready to go up to Camp IV, the highest before the summit, and they eventually got there. My daughters were at Camp II with the Sherpas, tightly packed into an ice cave to keep warm, preparing to make for Camp III.

In Camp IV there were now two climbers and only one Sherpa. Wangdi at Camp II was very uneasy and he at last decided that conditions were far from right, so he set out with another Sherpa to get the climbers down from Camp IV to safety before it was too late. But the avalanches began to roll before they reached the camp and they themselves were overwhelmed. Wangdi himself escaped, although he reached Camp I again in a bad way; the other Sherpa, his companion in the attempt to rescue the climbers, was lost, swept away by the avalanche. He was buried too deep to reach. Before he had set out for the highest camp, Wangdi had already ordered the evacuation of the rest and the girls were safely down at base by the time the avalanches broke loose. All night long, for hour after hour, the avalanches went on and on, roaring down the mountainsides, and there was nothing anybody could do about the missing women and their Sherpa up near the summit. When the weather eventually cleared a search was made to locate Camp IV, but the camp and its inhabitants had vanished without trace. The winds had been appalling; speeds of 100 miles an hour, it is said. They had literally torn the tent and the climbers from the mountain and hurled them into the depths, burying them in the avalanching snow for ever. It is the only explanation, for the search was continued for a week without result. Then the weather cleared again and the mountain shone out bright and clear in the blue sky as the expedition turned and left for Kathmandu. Had they started for their mountain a little later than they actually did, who knows that they might have succeeded without trouble? But that is the luck of the weather in that part of the world.

As for my daughters and their cousin, they were unharmed, having got to base as Wangdi had ordered. Thus two lady climbers lost their lives, Claude Kogan and Claudine Van der Stratten, as well as two Sherpas, Narbu and Chewang. Pem-Pem and Nima were very sad that their one and only great expedition had ended in such tragedy. Both had reached a height of 22,000 feet, which is good for a first climb. Since those days they have done a little rock-climbing, but no real mountaineering. They are now both married with children, and they both have careers. But had the weather on Cho Oyu been good throughout, possibly they might on their first venture have followed their leader to the top. Nobody knows. To me it would have been fine had they done so.

8: TIME OFF

I have sometimes been asked why it is that, since our return from Everest in 1953, I have not taken part in any other major climbing expedition. Certainly, I would have liked to have done, especially in some of the Indian expeditions, though in fact I was not invited. But the real answer is quite simple. The season for expeditions in the Himalaya coincides with the time when I am busy with the affairs of the Institute, very probably looking after my groups of students up in the training centre in Sikkim. And the expeditions leave the mountains alone at the same time as it becomes impossible for us to carry on with the instructional courses, because the weather has broken and the mountains are in no condition for climbing of any kind.

Every year training starts at the beginning of March and continues until the middle of June, with basic and advanced courses in progress at the same time, and a ladies' course as well. Field training is at a stop from the middle of June till the beginning of September because of the monsoon and the condition of the mountains. But during that time the Institute remains open and provides adventure courses for schoolboys. In fact, there is only one month in which the Institute is completely closed : February, and this is the time when I can look after my own home and enjoy the company of my family and friends.

February, moreover, is the month of the Sherpa new year festival and the children are all at home from school and I have them around me. The new year is celebrated by Sherpas and Tibetans at the same time and in the same way because we are all really one people. We call it Lohsar and it is quite different from the Nepalese new year, known as Bisket, and is held at a different time. But the Buddhists in Nepal who come from Tibet, Sikkim and Bhutan do celebrate our Lohsar festival in February and perform a grand parade 'of a thousand lights' around the great stupa at Bodhnath, near Kathmandu, at midnight, chanting prayers as they go. As for Darjeeling, it has many festivals because so many different peoples have settled there, each bringing its own traditions; they make the town gay all the year through.

I am away from home for such a large part of the year while I am working for the Institute -apart from my long journeys abroad, which are also of importance to both the Institute and the country—that I look forward to the month at home with special pleasure, with my wife and children, my many friends, my dogs and my horse, and of course the house. So I have tried not to be away at this time, though occasionally this was not possible. And even when I am not teaching in the mountains or lecturing at the Institute, there is other work to do and there are many visitors to show around and explain the work we are trying to do. Visitors come from all parts of the world, some merely curious, but some seeking for help. The curious ones take up quite a lot of time; they come full of questions and wanting me to tell all the old stories over and over again. And they expect to see me. But that is what I am there for. Many others come for special advice, for advice in planning expeditions, wanting to know about weather and equipment, seeking help in securing porters and Sherpas for their journey. The training of Sherpas for just this sort of thing has been such a special responsibility at the Institute that we are naturally happy to help.

As the rest of my book will show, however, I have found many opportunities to travel, especially during the early years after Everest, when the Institute had not got going to full capacity, and in later years when these journeys were either at official request or had a certain official value. Leave was specially granted then, whether it was for promoting Darjeeling tea in America or visiting Russian climbing clubs to tell them what we had achieved at HMI. The longer journeys came later, while in the early years travelling was mostly confined to Europe, visiting old climbing friends and mountaineering organisations in Switzerland, Britain, France, Italy, Austria, Germany—and attending conferences and reunions.

One of the first of these visits was very early in 1955 when, after a brief and private visit to England I went on to France to stay with Lionel Terray in Chamonix. This was my first, but not my only, visit to the Mont Blanc region and Lionel showed me some of the beauties of those mountains under winter conditions, with their needle-like summits plastered with snow and ice; I did no serious climbing, though we explored quite a bit. Terray, who had been a member of the expedition that had conquered Annapurna—a climb that in 1950 really started off the succession of great Himalayan ascents—had when I saw him not long returned from a reconnaissance of Makalu with other French climbers; Makalu is one of the great giants of the Himalaya, and soon after our meeting in Chamonix, Terray and his comrades went out again and conquered it, he being one of the first pair of climbers to get to the top. Later still he did some more magnificent ascents in the Himalaya—including Jannu, for which I arranged the Sherpa party which included some of the best high altitude Sherpas available. The Sherpas and I actually went down to Biratnagar to meet the Frenchmen and I was able to wish them luck and success. Lionel also made some spectacular ascents in the southern Andes (especially Mount Fitzroy in Patagonia) and in Alaska, and his film of the Andean ascents was a prize-winner at Trento.

At the time of my visit to Chamonix in 1955 the townspeople gave me a great welcome and an honorary citizenship of Chamonix.

Lionel Terray was killed ten years later by a fall while climbing in the mountains of his own country. His climbing companion died with him.

From Chamonix I went on to Italy at the invitation of another great mountaineer, Achille Compagnoni, a professional guide like Terray and the conqueror in 1954 of K2, the world's second highest mountain, 28,253 feet high. He was forty at that time, the same age as myself when I got to the top of Everest. His companion in the ascent was Lino Lacedelli; the climb was done in extremely low temperatures and the sun was already close to setting when they left the summit. Much of the descent was done by starlight and the help of an electric torch which was soon exhausted. There were a number of dangerous slips, and on one occasion Compagnoni fell completely out of control, though he ended up in soft snow. This was indeed a very great success.

It was on the visit to Compagnoni in Italy that I at last learned to ski properly. I had already done some skiing in Kashmir at the beginning of the war when I was working with Colonel White of the Chitral Scouts and we were moving about a great deal around the Northwest Frontier territory. Colonel White took me on a number of private trips when time allowed and this included my first experience of skis. I enjoyed skiing right from the start, though after that I got no chance to become really competent for another fifteen years. Compagnoni gave me that chance.

With me in 1955 were my two daughters and my niece. Compagnoni took us for fifteen days to Monte Bondone, a fine piece of skiing country very close to Trento, where I was the guest of the city and its mayor, Signor Piccoli. The Piccolis provided all four of us with complete ski kits and arranged for a very experienced instructor for the girls. Compagnoni says that at first I was not a good skier. It is not surprising, since I had not skied for very many years. But he says that I had an aptitude for the sport and I learnt very quickly. I certainly enjoyed every minute. Then from Monte Bondone our friend took us all to Cervinia, on the Italian side of the Matterhorn, where we were his guests at his own hotel—for he is a hotel-keeper as well as a professional mountain guide—and there we continued skiing for another ten days in March in the most impressive mountain country with famous and beautiful summits all around us.

On one occasion we went by lift to the Plateau Rosa which lies in the high pass between the Matterhorn and the Breithorn, two very fine mountains on the frontier, and the view both north and south over the snow-covered ranges was astonishing, and I remembered the stories I had been told of the Matterhorn and its history. That year I did not go down to Zermatt; in fact, I did not visit Zermatt for many years. But we all skied down again to Cervinia from the Plateau.

Since those days I have continued skiing in many parts of the world and never miss a chance, in Switzerland, Austria, France, Russia and Japan, where I was the guest of Japanese friends at Saporo in the year before the Olympic winter games there. By invitation I have toured many winter sport stations in France and Austria as well as Switzerland—especially in February 1958, when I again had the three girls with me. And in the spring of 1973, on the invitation of Carl Weber, I took part in the famous Engadin ski marathon, starting from St Moritz and covering over twenty-five miles cross-country. Hundreds and hundreds of skiers took part, but I was the only representative of India and Nepal. However, I had little experience of langlauf skiing and I was really not properly equipped for it and I was forced to give up without completing the course. Achille Compagnoni was also in St Moritz at that time. From there I went on to ski in other parts of Switzerland—Arosa and Grindelwald, and I think I rate now as a fairly competent skier, not on a competitive level, but just for pleasure. Daku learned to ski in Arosa during the same winter as my marathon attempt.

I met Achille Compagnoni again in 1956 when I was invited to attend the festival of mountain films at Trento, when many famous climbers were present, including Lord Hunt and Lionel Terray. Afterwards we returned to India by way of Athens, stopping only briefly to meet members of the Greek Alpine Club and to visit the Acropolis and its wonderful ruins. I was in Italy, in 1957, too, as Compagnoni's guest in Cervinia, after which we travelled together to Rome and in October I was received in private audience by Pope John XXIII. So I had now been received by two of the great spiritual leaders of the world, the Pope and the Dalai Lama, both of whom had shown a great interest in mountaineering. The Trento festival that year was especially memorable; the autumn weather was splendid and the excursion up the Lake of Garda was truly beautiful. An enormous number of films was shown, well over 100, from twenty lands or more. Afterwards I went to stay with Raymond Lambert once more, followed by a tour of Switzerland, returning to Geneva early in November. And I was back again in Geneva in February of the following year, with Pem-Pem, Nima and Doma, before beginning a tour of French and Austrian ski resorts at the invitation of official organisations in those countries.

And so the first ten years after Everest were busy not only with building up the work of the Institute but with much travelling to and fro between India and Europe. Apart from the journeys I have just described, I visited London again, for the centenary dinner of the Alpine Club, where all the great climbers of Britain, including most of the 1953 Everest team, were gathered all together to celebrate. But the really long and distant travelling was still to come, the journeys that took me to parts of the world I had never even thought of before—or even after—the Everest climb, but which were opened to me mainly as a result of our achievement then and the friends I have collected during my climbing career, very many of them since 1953. This is one of the most satisfying things about my many visits to Europe and farther afield: the unending friendship of other mountaineers everywhere, their continuous kindness and generosity always, even after long intervals. In almost all cases the only language my friends and I could talk together was English, my own English being not always so very good and theirs sometimes not much better. Strangely, this did not turn out to be a very great problem, and wherever I travelled, in Italy or France, in Switzerland or

Greece, we managed very well and there were no serious misunderstandings.

During all these years the work of HMI went on as the numbers of our students grew and our reputation spread, and I was more and more involved in my work there, so that for a year or two my travelling was more restricted. Groups of students had to be lectured to at headquarters and taken in turn up into Sikkim for field training and brought back again, taught and watched and judged. My time was very full.

Ang Lahmu remained in Darjeeling during most of the journeys I have described. Unlike Daku, my third wife, whom I had not yet met, Ang Lahmu had no love for long-distance travel, and the London visit of 1953, with Pem-Pem and Nima to make it a family party, was the only big journey she ever undertook. Meanwhile, in the later 'fifties I had the company of my growing daughters on quite a few of my travels, when they were invited to skiing holidays and mountaineering festivals by my ever-generous hosts.

9: RUSSIAN ADVENTURE; WEDDING IN SIKKIM

The year 1963 was for me a particularly busy one and I visited so many countries in such rapid succession that there are times when my memory becomes a little confused and I tend to get events in the wrong order. Until Everest I had not travelled far afield; the expedition to the Hindu Kush with Mr and Mrs Smeeton was my farthest from Darjeeling and that was in 1939. But after our return from the conquest of Everest came my first long journey: to England and Europe with Ang Lahmu and our two young daughters. After that I seemed to be always flying somewhere. You get into a plane and then, a few hours later, you are somewhere else, thousands of miles away; then you get into another plane and in a few hours more you are again in another quite different place. But by 1963 I had already made quite a few long journeys, yet never beyond Europe; in this year, however, I was continually on the move and during the spring and summer visited Russia—Moscow, Leningrad, the Caucasus, Tashkent, the Tien Shan mountains, Alma Ata—then Sikkim for a wedding, Australia, Singapore, Switzerland, England. For some months I had little time at home.

From Delhi in February I flew direct to Moscow across the roof of the world with a brief stop at Tashkent. In Delhi, when I left, the weather was quite warm, so that I was dressed in my usual Indian warm-weather clothing. When I got to Moscow the whole world was white; you could see from the plane that the land was all under deep snow, stretching as far as you could see. As I left the plane at Moscow airport I was very cold indeed. How I shivered! My Russian hosts, however, were quick to provide me with a big Russian hat and a Russian coat to keep me warm.

I was in Russia for a week and during my stay was presented with the Russian medal for outstanding achievement in sport; I believe I am the only non-Russian to receive it, or was at that time. The President was away from Moscow and although I saw his residence in the Kremlin I could not meet him. I was taken to Lenin's tomb, of course, and saw the long line of Russians waiting in the cold to do the same thing, and I was shown more historical places than I can remember. Then I was taken to Leningrad, where I gave a talk in English to their alpine club. After that we flew down to the Caucasus mountains.

This was quite a short visit and it gave me no time for real mountaineering. But I went with some Russian climbers to Mount Elbruz, a fine mountain of over 18,000 feet and I tramped up as far as the last refuge, about five hundred feet from the top, where we were stopped by bad weather. In spite of the height and the deep snow—for this was winter- this was nothing more serious than very strenuous walking. No real mountaineering; nothing difficult at all, not even close to the top.

About half-way up on the first day's march we came to a small and comfortable hut. Outside stood a very beautiful Russian girl with a sweet smile for me, and it was then that I felt sorry that I did not know how to speak her language. She gave me hot soup and it was very good. The day's march ended at the refuge close to the summit. It was a big hut and most comfortable. The weather was good on arrival and the sun was shining brightly, and we were all most excited about setting out for the top the next morning. But at midnight a terribly high wind began to blow, which continued after daybreak so that it was impossible to start. We stayed in the hut for the day, unable to move, and the next morning was just as bad. I asked if we could stay for another day, just for the weather to clear; the chance to reach the top of one of the highest of Russian mountains might not come again. But my Russian companion, who was also my interpreter, told me that in the Elbruz region, when such weather starts it goes on for a long time; so we had to pack up and go down.

We went down on skis and it was a very exciting descent. We quickly lost sight of each other in the blizzard and the blowing snow. Besides what was actually falling, a lot more snow was swept up from the surface by the gale and was swirling around us in the air. Everything was white, the sky, the earth, my companions. We could not see for more than fifteen yards ahead and badly at that, and we were all skiing in different directions, some this way, some that, sometimes together and sometimes alone. It was quite strange and very difficult. Fortunately, there were neither glaciers nor rocks to worry about.

My Russian friends seemed sure of the way, so I kept on, following them as best I could, although I did not see them much of the time, until after about three thousand feet we were all together again. Still, I enjoyed this trip, for even if we could not see much that was around us and the wind filled the ski tracks ahead as fast as they were made, the powder snow was marvellous and smooth. I was sorry I had not been to the top and that I had seen so little, for I am not likely to be there again.

At last we came to the valley, where there was a hot spring of mineral water which the Russians told me is a very good medicine. They told me that they bottled it and sent it to every part of Russia. They drank a lot of it themselves, so I swallowed two large jugfuls before we moved on.

Our next mountain in the Caucasus was Ushba, about 15,400 feet high, but quite different from Elbruz. Not as high but sharply pointed and very steep. To me it was a little like the Matterhorn, although it has two clearly separated summits. It is beautiful but difficult, though it has, of course, been climbed many times, the first time by an Englishman in the last century. It has a permanent snow covering and the ascent route is by a steep ridge with large cornices, but when I was there conditions were very wintry and quite unsuitable for any attempt at climbing. All we could do was walk up about half-way.

I saw many other mountains in the Caucasus, including one that was said to be unclimbed, but that seems hard to believe. I would have liked to stay there for a month at least and to have climbed some of the many beautiful summits with my Russian climbing friends; they seemed to be good climbers, most friendly, jolly and hospitable, like all the Russian people I met. Again it was just not possible to stay; we had to move on, and we went to Tiflis.

At that time, I 963, it seemed that all the climbing material I saw was imported, but a lot of time has passed since then and things have probably changed. All the towns in the Caucasus, and the villages as well, had schools of climbing and skiing, even at that time, and all mountain sports were very popular. The people love their mountains. The Georgians are gay and they drink a great deal—everything and anything alcoholic, vodka and wine in huge quantities. Too much for me, since at that time I did not touch any kind of strong drink, not even beer. Only soft drinks. It was Lord Hunt who had warned me against alcohol; once you start, he told me, it is difficult to stop. Leave it alone, he said. I have not left it entirely alone, but I do not normally drink spirits—except for a little rakshi when I am visiting in the Himalayan villages.

On this trip I was entirely alone among my hosts. I had no English or Indian companions and I could not, of course, speak Russian. So we had to talk together in a sort of English, but we made ourselves understood. The Georgians appear to be hardworking people, in spite of their heavy drinking and gay behaviour; their land is beautiful, rich and fertile, and there is fruit everywhere.

My first book, the one Jim Ullman wrote for me, is very popular in Russia I found. But so far I have made no money from it at all, because the Russians until very recently have not recognised any copyright in foreign books, nor paid anything to a foreign author for translating his work into Russian and selling it in no matter what numbers. I have been told that this situation has now changed and the Russians have reached an agreement with other countries to put this situation right, except that they will still pay nothing for the books they have already sold but only those sold as from the date of their agreement. Well, we shall see. Up till now I have received nothing, and it looks as though I shall see nothing for all those books of mine that have been sold during the past twenty years.

From Georgia I flew to Tashkent and visited its climbing club. I was given a great reception and was made an honorary member. I was also given a Lenin medal. Then I flew on to Alma Ata so that I could at least see a little of the fine mountains that stand distantly between them and China. Very high they are and little known to any but Russians. Time again was short and I had only three days to spend there. Distances are great and there was no chance to do any climbing, as I would have liked. Instead we had a two day trek, carrying our food and our tents, just like the tourists do in Nepal. I can only say that the scenery was magnificent and the people rather like my own and most hospitable. I was made a member of the Alma Ata climbing club and was given yet another big reception.

In this region they grow a very special apple; it is seedless. And since I was now on my way home I took a basket of these apples as a present for Pandit Nehru, with which he was very pleased.

In Tashkent, where I stayed for a little while on my way home, I met the Russian climber who was reported in the foreign press to have seen the abominable snowman during an expedition in the Pamirs the previous year. So I asked him what it was he had seen. He said the report in the newspapers was untrue; that at a high altitude one night they had in fact been disturbed by a creature they had been unable to identify. Most probably it was a bear, he said, for in the Pamirs they have brown bears that are quite big. But it was not a yeti. They had never seen one, nor any trace of one. The disturber was certainly not human, or even sub-human.

I am always being asked about the yeti, the abominable snowman, especially since the ascent of Everest, and wherever I go, wherever I give a talk—in America, in Europe, in Australia -someone is certain to ask if I have seen one, or whether I believe in its existence. My answer now is no, to both questions. I have never seen one, nor have I seen any real sign of one. I am very interested in all kinds of animals, whether wild ones in the mountains or domestic animals in the civilised parts of the world, and I spent much of my earlier years alone in very high parts of the Khumbu region, apart from the climbing I have done during the past forty years, and I reckon that if anyone had seen a yeti it would have been me. But I have not.

A long time ago, high in the mountains above Khumbu, my own father once saw a strange creature, he said, not a human being but rather like a monkey; its hair was long and its colour was brown and white and it moved like an ape. Perhaps it was, in fact, a Himalayan ape. Now in my home valley the old people say that if anyone should happen to see such a creature he will have bad luck, so my father thought at once that he would fall ill. And of course he was very ill for three months.

Something also happened on an expedition which Eric Shipton took into Nepal. After it was all over he told me that one day at about 19,000 feet, above what later became Everest Camp I, he was alone when he saw a strange kind of animal a long way off. Soon afterwards he was taken ill and was unwell for a long time.

Since those days many people have been looking for the abominable snowman, but without success. There are always stories about him and there are so-called relics of him, but itis interesting that no one really does find him or meet him at close range, so that he can be described fairly clearly. As for the tales of occasional sightings, they always cause a stir, which is quite natural, but whenever I have asked the people of the mountains whom I know very closely whether they have seen the abominable snowman, it is clear they have not. But they add that if you do see one you will be very unlucky as a result.

Anyway, it seems very strange to me that in all these stories and rumours the yeti has always been alone. He never seems to have a family. He never seems to belong to a group. If someone has seen what is supposed to be strange footprints, there is never more than one animal involved. Now to survive in these remote places in very difficult conditions there must be more than one of them; there must be a family of yetis somewhere, otherwise they would soon die out. And if there was a group capable of having a continual supply of young ones to keep their kind going, they would surely leave a fairly clear trace of themselves. They would have to live somewhere, they would have to create shelter for themselves, they would have to eat and leave rubbish behind of some kind. But they never have. And what would they live on anyway in the wild regions where they are supposed to have been seen? There is nothing eatable there.

I have kept an open mind on this subject for a very long time, but it is now my opinion that the snowman does not exist. The tales will go on for ever, all the same, because people like a mystery, and this is a good one.

Now I was weighed down by all the medals I had been given, so I flew back to Moscow and from there to Delhi and Calcutta, because I had soon to be in Gangtok, the capital of Sikkim, for the royal wedding. I had been invited to attend by the royal family, whom I had known well for many years. I have spent a lot of time in Sikkim and I have always been on good terms with the family and the officials. The royal family—which has recently been deposed—is of Tibetan origin like myself, and our links have been most friendly. In March 1963 the Chogyal, the Crown Prince as he was then, was to marry the American girl Hope Cooke, whom I had already met, and I was to be present during all the celebrations.

I had first to get from Delhi to Calcutta, but because of the large number of diplomats and official guests all flying in the same direction for the same celebrations it was difficult to get a seat on the planes, but I eventually succeeded. At Calcutta we had to change planes and I spent the night there. The nearest airport to Gangtok is in India, south of Darjeeling, itself a taxi journey of three hours away. From Darjeeling another taxi ride through the mountains completes the journey. But just as we were ready to take off from Calcutta early in the morning the cabin was suddenly filled with smoke and we were all ordered out in a hurry for fear of fire. Half an hour later we were all back in the same plane, though I admit that I was a little anxious.

Sikkim is a very small and beautiful land, no bigger, and with a smaller number of people, than an English county, I should think. I know it well, quite apart from the several times each year that I take my students up into the training areas and back again. I have been there many times privately, on foot as well as by

64

car, for it is not a great distance to walk for people used to Himalayan travel. Sherpas in Darjeeling often walk to Khumbu and back merely to see their relations, and that is very much farther than to Gangtok. In the south of Sikkim, on the borders of India, are jungle-covered hills, warm and full of flowers, tropical flowers lower down and in the higher levels very much the same sorts of flowers as you might find in the Alps. It is through Darjeeling that the only practical approach exists today, because political conditions make entry through Tibet impossible; it would be difficult enough anyway, since on this northern frontier lies a horseshoe of high and shining mountains with only a few passes, all, with one exception, difficult. All the same, invaders and migrating tribes came through them into Sikkim a few hundred years ago.

The mountains are a magnificent sight, especially Kangchenjunga, which forms the western frontier. These mountains have a special place in the beliefs and the traditions of the people, who are of Tibetan origin and Buddhist. The mountains are not only the thrones of the gods; they are sometimes the gods themselves, as their names often make clear. Kangchenjunga, which they say means 'The Great Glacier of the Five Treasures', is the symbol, more or less, of the state of Sikkim. The land is full of great Buddhist monasteries, some of them very big indeed and quite old, like the Sanga Chelling, Rupti, Dupti, Tashiding and Talang gompas, and many others. And they all contain beautiful pieces of Buddhist religious art.

Most of the people are Nepalis or of Nepalese origin. The earliest inhabitants were Lepchas, but then came the invasion of the Bhutias from Tibet, who from then on ruled the land while the Lepchas remained very few. The recently deposed king and the upper classes are all Bhutias, even if their subjects are nearly all Nepalis; they call themselves Kazis, which means 'the land lords'. The history of Sikkim is very short, only a few hundred years, and the story goes that in the early days, when there was no king in the land, three lamas came over from Tibet on a pilgrimage because they had been told that what we now call Sikkim was a very holy place. One of these lamas, called Lapsen Chimbo, had a dream that a king would be found who would be a boy delivering milk in the early morning from a full can. So early next morning the lamas sent men out to search for the boy and he was found, just as the dream said, carrying a full can of milk. His name was Namgyal and he was created king. This was the first crowning ever to take place in Sikkim and the place where it occurred was Yoksam—the very same Yoksam through which all our students pass on their way up from Darjeeling to their training area. The name means 'the three lamas'. The other two lamas were Rathok Rinzin and Thingong, who was a Lepcha.

Gangtok is still small but growing rapidly. It stands at about 5,000 feet. The people there are very gentle, simple and hospitable. Whenever I visit the town the people come from everywhere to greet me and to invite me to drink chang with them in their houses.

The wedding was a colourful affair and I was present throughout the celebrations. Many hundreds of lamas, perhaps a thousand or more, chanted prayers and blessed the young couple, Palden Thondup and Hope Cooke. The whole way from the town to the palace gompa was brilliantly decorated. The Prince himself was dressed for the wedding by the lamas of the Pemayongtse monastery, the oldest in the land. The feasting lasted a week and almost every person in Sikkim was fed at public expense. A huge number of people from all over Sikkim were camped around the town and their tents, made of many cloths of many colours, were an astonishing sight. So were their garments, for they wore their very brightest traditional clothing, which added enormously to the gaiety of the scene. Many diplomats and a number of ambassadors were accommodated in the town. From end to end the mood was gay and the streets were thronged with visitors and vividly coloured.

I should add that quite recently the Prince whom I saw married, and who later became King -I was a guest at his coronation too—has lost his throne and the marriage too has broken up. The land of Sikkim is for all practical purposes part of the Indian state. In recent times there has been some unrest and I have been accidentally present at some of it. Modern conditions are spreading into the land, especially its capital, and roads are being built into the more remote places, places that until quite recently were very seldom visited by western people. There is a pad for helicopter landing in Gangtok and jeeps can be seen in many places which only a few years ago had been unchanged for centuries.

Among the European guests at this wedding was June Kirkwood, whom I had met in Darjeeling earlier, when I had shown her round the Institute a few years after, I think, it was founded. She, too, was friendly with the royal family and she knew Hope Cooke as well. I had met her again in Gangtok in 1961, when she was acting in a friendly capacity as a companion to the future queen—this was the occasion of her betrothal, as far as I can remember—when Hope was carrying out a number of official duties, like opening schools. I happened to be there at the time on one of my many unofficial visits and in the end escorted the two ladies back to Darjeeling on a journey that turned out to be far from pleasant. It is not normally a difficult drive; about four or five hours over a winding and occasionally hazardous track, full of hairpin bends. We used a jeep. First of all, from Gangtok you have to drop down to the Tista river, perhaps 2,000 feet below; then you have to climb about six or seven thousand feet on a narrow road that zigzags continuously with little or no protection on one side from a fall into space. Then you cross a pass at about 10,000 feet and descend afterwards to Darjeeling. When the weather is foggy, as it was on the night I escorted June and Hope Cooke, it can be quite worrying to negotiate this road, and it was extremely cold too.

It was on the long climb up from the Tista that June began to feel very unwell and then, just when we were near the pass, a tyre went flat. Although I know nothing about motors, I at least succeeded in getting the driver to work fast, so that we were not held up for very long. As soon as we were back in Darjeeling I went home with Pem-Pem, who had come to meet me, and I left the ladies to go to their hotel. I heard from June later that within half an hour she was dreadfully ill, never so ill, she said, in her life before or since. It was said that there had actually been an attempt, for political reasons, to poison Hope, by no one knows whom, but probably one of the palace cliques, and that she had been advised secretly what to eat and what not to eat during the ceremonial lunch before she left Gangtok. So Hope had no trouble afterwards, but June Kirkwood was in a very bad way for some hours and it looks as if she was the unintended victim of the plot, if there *was* a plot.

June Kirkwood left Darjeeling in 1962 and when the Gangtok wedding was due she was already living in Singapore, and when we met at the wedding she invited me to spend some time at her home on my way to and from Australia, a journey which I had to make quite soon.

When all the wedding celebrations were over many of the guests made a short stop in Darjeeling and quite a few came to see me. They were particularly interested in my dogs, since for many years I had been breeding these Tibetan terriers and had given some away to my friends in distant parts of the world. These dogs are known as Lhasa Absos. Some of my visitors after the wedding wanted a dog for themselves and asked me my price. But I replied that if they were very keen to own one then they were most welcome to take a dog away. So some got puppies of six months and some got older dogs, and away they went with people in the diplomatic service from France, Japan, Britain, Italy, Switzerland and elsewhere.

I had brought the original pair from Tibet when I had travelled there with Professor Tucci in 1948; they were given to me by the monks of the monastery of Ghangar. From these I bred and at one time I had as many as sixty-five.

I have been told that some Lhasa Absos (*abso* means long-haired) were taken into Britain a few years before the war by the wife of a diplomat who had lived in Lhasa. But they were little known in the West until very recently and partly as a result of the dogs I had given away to my visitors over the years. It has now been an officially recognised breed for quite a few years and can be seen at the main shows. There are descendants of my own dogs in many lands and when I was in Los Angeles in 1972 I was asked to act as a judge of the breed at a show there. In my view the entrants were, for the most part, too inbred; not enough of the breed had been available until then and there was no fresh blood. Now they are becoming more numerous, but still very expensive. In America in 1972 they were asking as much as $5,000 for a dog of good pedigree, and there was one advertised with a good pedigree for $15,000. That is a lot of money, and I now realise that if I had bred these Absos commercially instead of giving them away I could have been a rich man. I daresay that in Europe now they are a bit cheaper than in America in 1972.

However, I am not really interested in getting rich that way. And we Sherpas are superstitious about our dogs. We say that it is not good to sell your dog. In the Sherpa language the word for dog and the word for luck are the same: *tchu*. Therefore, if you sell your dog you sell your luck too. But if someone will keep a dog well and look after it, I will give a dog away.

When an international mountaineering meet took place in Darjeeling in 1973, even more of my Absos found new owners and went to Europe, America and even Japan with the climbing representatives from those lands. So now I have very few left, though I have recently acquired new parents to breed from, parents that I have bought from Tibetans who have found their way over the frontier. Albert Eggler, the Swiss climber, has one of the new generation; so has Heinrich Harrer, the author of *Seven Years in Tibet*. I took one to Achille Compagnoni, the Italian conqueror of K2, the second highest mountain in the world, when I visited him at his Italian home some years ago.

I am very fond of all animals and when I travel in other peoples' countries it is their animals that I especially want to see, domestic or wild. But I love dogs above all, and apart from my Absos I have a Tibetan mastiff. These mastiffs are quite ferocious and difficult to look after. They are big and powerful and cannot be left to run free. Certainly not in a town like Darjeeling; they could be too dangerous. Tibetan mastiffs are kept by some of the tea garden people up in the hills to look after their property. To me they are not dangerous; they are very handsome and make good watch-dogs. With this one beside my house in Tonga Road I am no longer troubled by the curious intruders who were a nuisance to me and my family in the past; they now keep well away.

10: AUSTRALIA, SINGAPORE, EUROPE

I was not at home for long in that early part of 1963, for I was no sooner back from the wedding in Gangtok than I had to prepare for a journey to Australia, the first I had taken in that part of the world. I had also been invited to visit Japan following the Australia tour, but this in the end did not prove possible and I had to wait another few years before the opportunity occurred again.

So in April, on the invitation of the Australian Adult Education Board, I made a twenty-one day visit to Tasmania, mainly taken up by a lecture tour, visiting schools, clubs and societies, during which, as elsewhere, I showed the Everest film and talked about the climb and about the work of the Institute. I was most interested by the Tasmanian way of life, which I found quite different from the life I had seen in Europe or any other place I had been till then. The fields and forests deeply impressed me, and so did the high standard of living of the Tasmanian people, the fine crops of fruit and the wonderful sheep and cattle, which I saw especially at the Hamilton show. And for the first time in my life I saw a kangaroo and made friends with some one morning at Lake St Clair.

The highlight of the visit, however, was the Easter mountaineering camp held in the Mount Field National Park. In 1960 Sir Edmund Hillary had been the principal guest at this camp, and the following year it had been George Lowe's turn. George, it will be remembered, had been one of the leading climbers in the 1953 Everest expedition; like Hillary a native of New Zealand, he had married one of Lord Runt's daughters. In 1963 they were living in South America, where George was a teacher. Now it was my turn at the Tasmanian camp.

The weather was not good. There were drifting mists and even a fall of snow on the first night, after about sixty campers had settled into the huts at Lake Dobson. The mountains in this part are not very high, not by Himalayan or Alpine standards, being only a little more than 4,000 feet, but they are wild and beautiful and each day was occupied with fairly strenuous walking through what is called 'the bush' to different parts of the inland plateau. Further snow fell at intervals throughout the stay, but the treks went on nevertheless. In the evenings there were talks and discussions on many aspects of bush-walking and mountaineering, in which I took a part. I described my Himalayan experiences to the campers and talked to them, as others did too, about mountain safety, of search and rescue operations, leadership and so on. As there was no question of mountaineering—properly speaking—at this camp, there was not much point in dealing with the practical aspects of climbing, so I kept what I had to say to general matters of adventuring in open country. We do run adventure courses at HMI in Darjeeling, so I had some real experience of these matters to pass on.

Although the camp site is not particularly far from Hobart, the main city, this was the beginning of the Australian winter and the snow that covered the ground there in April was quite thick. For many of the campers it was their first experience of such conditions, but it proved a very suitable background to the talks and discussions.

Then on the last night I was presented with a birthday cake, all iced and with a little Mount Everest on the top. It was not really my birthday, which was a month later, but my hosts had decided to advance the date a little so as to be able to make this presentation and to sing me the 'Happy Birthday' song. They also gave me a 'Jim Brown' bushwalker's slasher in a leather sheath, signed by every-one in the camp, and it was used to cut the cake.

On my way back from Tasmania I spent some time in other parts of Australia, some of it conducting a group of young people on a bush-walking course. Thus I saw quite a lot of the Australian bush which, though not real mountain country as I understand the word, is nevertheless very thick and wild. The leaders of these bush-walking courses each carry a whistle to keep contact with other groups. For me it was quite a new experience; this was the beginning of their winter and snow was beginning to fall in a few high places.

I 'lectured' in a number of cities, including Sydney and Melbourne, to schools, colleges and clubs: very much the same short talk as I have given all over the world since then—and before—about the ascent of Everest mainly and our work at HMI, together with a showing of the film of the ascent. I have since been told that I gave as many as ten of these talks a day, which sounds a lot and I cannot swear to that figure because I have long lost count. I only know that it was very many and that at the end of the tour I was quite exhausted, because I really find that speaking in public is a strain, even today when I have done so much of it. I began to feel too that I was finding little that was new to say and that I was therefore becoming a bit repetitive. This might have been embarrassing, except that I found my audiences always attentive and interested. They asked many ques-tions, though the same old ones about the abominable snowman and who got to the top first turned up as usual everywhere.

On the homeward journey I stopped at Darwin, where I had planned to remain for a few days; but it was too hot there and I was always pursued by clouds of mosquitoes. I did not like Darwin at all, so in the end I stayed for one night only and left the next morning because of the number of bites I had suffered. A reception had been arranged for me, though very few people came to it, so there was nothing embarrassing about my departure earlier than scheduled.

As for Australia as a whole, I was impressed by its size and the thinness of the population; its high standard of living was clear to see; the houses all seemed to me to have fine gardens and there was a great quantity of fruit every-where. I was especially interested by the unusual wild life, as well as by the huge numbers of sheep and cattle. I enjoyed their cheese and milk. If I can find in any country plenty of good cheese, milk and fruit, I can be a very satisfied man. These were the things that caught my attention, but in one thing I was disappointed. In my young days I had been told that in Australia there was a miniature species of tiger that was very rare, but though I asked about them everywhere nobody seemed to know anything about it and I was certainly never shown one. I had also heard when I was young about a bush bear, and this too I never saw.

On the outward journey to Australia I had stayed briefly with the Kirkwoods in Singapore, and on my way back I stayed with them again, this time for rather longer, about two weeks. June showed me a great deal of the city. It was very hot there, and I remember especially the great beauty of the orchids. When I arrived at Singapore I was entertained to dinner at the old airport, now used for this sort of occasion, by the People's Youth Association, and was welcomed as we turned in at the drive by the famous lion dance, a traditional and highly-coloured performance usually reserved for festivals, holidays and distinguished visitors.

June also took me to Kuala Lumpur to meet the Tunku Abdul Rahman. This visit was both amusing and exhausting. To get there and back in the same day and do all we planned to do meant getting up at a very early hour and catching the first plane of the day. Then, sitting in this plane while travelling at about 20,000 feet, I was attracted by the sight of crowds of little boats immediately beneath us along the shore. I had made many flights before, over sea and land, but on this occasion I was suddenly struck by the great emptiness between me and the tiny boats below; so I turned to June and said, 'Just look at that crowd of boats!' But June, who does not like looking out of aeroplane windows, glanced briefly and said simply 'Yes', turning her eyes away again. Yet to me it seemed quite odd that many times I had walked along at just this same height on my own two feet and had thought nothing of it; now I could not take my eyes away.

When we got to Kuala Lumpur I found that first of all we had to visit a film set and watch the making of a film. Nobody had warned us of this when we set out from Singapore, but there was no dodging it. An American company was filming a curious story in which a whole Malaysian village had been specially built just to be burned down. To me this seemed completely crazy. It was a beautiful village, all made of new timber, and it must have cost an enormous sum of money. I thought then that there must be in Malaysia many people who would have liked a whole new village specially built for them to live in. The waste was dreadful. It was wicked.

The morning was very hot indeed; we were not prepared for such a visit, and for an hour or more we stood around without even an umbrella to give us shade in order to watch the whole crazy business of filming. In that blazing sunshine I felt angry for June's sake at such a lack of consideration. Then we were all lined up for photographs, though I had no wish to be photographed with all these people I did not know and would never see again. The film stars themselves seemed very ordinary people, not good-looking at all and I could not find them interesting, and the same goes for all those men, directors or producers, whatever they are called, walking endlessly about and organising people. I desperately wanted to get away; so, I am sure, did June. But there was no escape.

We were taken to lunch at a club. When I am abroad, and especially in places like this club, what to eat is always a difficulty; I cannot read the menus, and even if I could I would not understand them. So I have to depend on the advice of others entirely and in this case it was June who guided me. Afterwards we were taken to a building site—a school in the making, I believe—but I did not understand much of what was going on and again hoped we could escape. Everyone was wandering about and having a lot of time to spend on doing practically nothing.

It was at this moment that someone discovered that I had no present for the Tunku, whom I was about to meet. Anyway I had not known till the day before that I was going to meet him at all, and certainly knew nothing about this ritual of present giving. Then someone remembered that there was a Tibetan horn in one of the oriental art shops near by and dashed off to buy it, so that I should not be empty-handed. In good time I had a present for the Tunku after all, supposedly straight from Tibet. Eventually we were taken into his presence and for a while I sat beside him and talked in English. He asked me many questions about my mountaineering life and adventures, and said that although there were no mountains in Malaysia he wished the people could take part in trekking and rock-climbing and similar outdoor activities which might have beneficial results in terms of leadership and initiative. I believe that some time after this talk a club for these activities was organised.

Then I gave the Tunku the horn from Tibet, with which he seemed delighted, and he gave me a present in exchange, a Malaysian sword. And that was that. At least we hoped that this was all, but found we were expected to a party, about which we knew nothing at all. It looked as if I was to be the party's attraction, which did not please me a bit. We were kept hanging about in a very hot room, waiting for people to arrive, and our clothes were sticking to us, and we were very uncomfortable indeed. I kept saying to June, 'I don't like this. Let's go. ' But we had to go on shaking hands, though we were extremely tired. So I made out that it was most important that we should leave then and there to catch a plane, and this we did before the party really got going, and saw at least one ambassador arriving as we vanished. Our host was not very pleased.

The ordeal was not over yet, for on the same plane was a prominent Malaysian politician who had had, I think, too much to drink already, for he kept banging me on the back and addressing me as 'the hero of Asia', insisting that I accompany him to a meeting he was addressing that evening. This was dangerous, but with June's help I managed to get away. The next morning, when I saw him in his office he was sober and presented me with a couple of vases which I really did not want.

I think it was in Singapore that I travelled in a boat for the first time in my life. It was a high-speed naval motor launch and I remember that we were piped aboard. So long as I could see the shore I found the trip interesting, but as soon as we were in the open sea and travelling fast I lost interest entirely. For I have no feeling for machines or engineering, and speed even today is something that does not mean much to me. A boat—or an aeroplane—is only something for getting me from one place to another, and not a thing of interest in itself or of any importance otherwise, any more than how it works or how fast it goes. The things that hold me are people and animals, mountains and flowers; with these I know where I am and they give me satisfaction. Also, I prefer to be doing something—walking, riding, climbing, talking—always with living creatures and with people. But sitting in a plane, or a boat or a motor-car, except if I want to get somewhere, is not in itself a pleasure; it is almost a waste of time. I get restless with so much inactivity. The same goes for television, of which I have seen only a little; I cannot sit just looking. I want to do something, if it is only making tea.

On the other hand I get great happiness from family life. I love my children; I love to be with them and to join in their games, and when they were young—some still are—I spent much of what spare time I had with them. And I like to learn about things, not about machinery of course, but fishing for instance, and how people look after their cattle in other countries, or raise and improve their crops, and all such matters.

While I was in Singapore I visited the Gurkha regiment in its barracks, and had to record a broadcast at the radio station there; and while I was waiting my turn in the studio found myself sitting with Acker Bilk, who said to me: 'You have climbed the highest mountain in the world, and I have reached the highest note. ' I also tried my hand at golf: it was amusing to get the ball into the hole, but I found it hard to believe that so many people could spend so much time in such a fashion.

I went to the dentist too—not because I had to, but because he, the dentist, wanted to look at my teeth! This is the first and only time I have ever sat in a dentist's chair. He did in fact find one tiny cavity, which he filled, but he said that otherwise my teeth were as unworn as those of a ten-year-old. A lot of people in the Western world have remarked on my teeth, and I have therefore wondered what it is that I have done to keep them as they are. I believe that constant brushing is bad; it wears down the surface of the teeth in the end. Instead I use plain salt, rubbing it around the teeth with the ball of my finger. I have never used anything else and I think there is nothing better. My diet is nothing remarkable; it is common to the East. I eat little meat; I like vegetables and fruit and rice;

I eat no sweets, though I take sugar in my tea; and of dairy produce I am very fond.

It was only a few days after my return from Australia and Singapore that I was off again, this time to Switzerland and London and Wales. For this was the tenth anniversary of the great climb and there were celebrations to which I had been invited. They coincided, moreover, with the great American ascent of Everest by the West Ridge and the first traverse of the mountain—ascending by the one ridge and descending by the other. It had been a tremendous performance, and Gombu, my nephew and instructor at HMI, had made his first ascent of the mountain on that occasion. He made a second ascent later.

The British celebrations took place first at Pen-y-Gwryd in North Wales, and many members of the 1953 expedition were there as well as some from the 1955 Kangchenjunga team. There was no real climbing, but I did a lot of walking, especially with the Hunts, and I can record having added Snowdon and Tryfan to my bag of summits, though they were both reached by perfectly safe paths. At Pen-y-gwryd I met Chris Bonnington for the first time; I met him again twelve years later when I was accompanying a party of Italian film-makers in Khumbu and Bonnington was on his way back from the magnificent conquest of the south-west face of Everest, and I had this chance to offer him my congratulations.

In London later, at the end of May, the old film of the first conquest of Everest was shown again at the Central Hall, Westminster, to a combined gathering of the Alpine Club and the Royal Geographical Society. The Duke of Edinburgh was there, and I was on the platform too, to say a few words to the audience about the pleasure it gave me to be there with my old comrades and about my appreciation of their friendship through the years. The Chinese had sent to London their own film of their alleged ascent by the northern route, but it was not convincing. There was no picture of the actual summit. What they showed as the summit looked to me more like Chang La. Since then a Chinese expedition really has reached the summit from the Tibetan side, where my own first trips to Everest took place.

The Swiss celebrations which followed took place at Meiringen at the middle of June. All the members of the British 1953 expedition were invited as well as those of the two Swiss expeditions of 1952 and the successful one of 1956. Dr Feuz had sent me an invitation and amongst the many people present were Lord Hunt and the British Everest veteran Professor Odell, also my old friends Dr Wyss-Dunant, Hofstetter, Asper, Ernst Reiss and especially Raymond Lambert, whom it was a great joy to see again. It was a very happy reunion. On one day we all walked over the Grosse Scheideck from Rosenlaui to First with the great north face of the Eiger in full view, and on another we climbed the Kleiner-

and Grosser-Simmelistock, which I had actually done before when training at Dr Glatthard's school in Rosenlaui. I remember that Lord Hunt and Albert Eggler were on one rope, I was on another with Ernst Schmied, and there were other pairs. It was all free climbing and very good fun, just two on a rope and for me a great experience. On another day we all went skiing, though it was already mid-summer, or nearly so.

Then at the very last moment we were joined by some of the American Everest team on their way home, after the West Ridge ascent. They could not stay with us long, because they had to hurry home where they were to meet President Kennedy as soon as they arrived. And so, after a very happy holiday, climbing some mountains, meeting old comrades and friends, a reception at the Indian Embassy and a party with the Nepalese consul in Switzerland, the celebrations came to an end.

Albert Eggler, one of the Swiss climbers of Everest, came out to India that summer on behalf of the Swiss Red Cross in connection with Tibetan refugees, about whom the Swiss have for long had a great concern. He came up to Darjeeling, of course, and he was given accommodation at the Institute. We met frequently during his stay; he came to my home, naturally, and he met my family, including Ang Lahmu and Daku.

On my journey to Europe I had taken with me two of my Lhasa Abso puppies, one for Lionel Terray, the French conqueror of Annapurna, and the other for Albert Eggler. Unfortunately they had been taken sick with distemper in New Delhi, but they recovered and I got them to their destination. Later, both died in road accidents. It was very sad, but ten years later I gave Albert Eggler another puppy and this one has survived to become a very devoted companion to this day.

From Switzerland, when the celebrations were over, I moved on to Austria to visit the climbing school run by Fritz Moravec, where I spent a week, taking his standard climbing course, observing the Austrian climbing techniques then being used and especially the new material they were using, much of which we later acquired for the Institute. Visits to climbing schools outside India are, of course, extremely useful to me, enabling the Institute to keep up to date in every way, though at that time our ability to import foreign-made material was rather restricted. Things are rather easier now and we even manufacture some of our own, though the demand is too limited for this to apply to every piece of equipment. Moravec's course was a short one and lasted only a week, at the end of which I was given his badge and certificate. Fritz Moravec is especially successful in introducing children to the joys of climbing; this is one of his specialities.

From Austria I moved into Germany to visit Paul Bauer, the famous German climber who had done some very remarkable climbing in the Himalaya a generation earlier, especially a nearly successful ascent of Nanga Parbat—the 'German Mountain'—in the year before the war, as well as some explorations in Sikkim two years earlier, when he had ascended Siniolchu, Simva and Nepal Peak. As far back as 1929 he had led an attempt on Kangchenjunga and reached a point above 24,000 feet before giving up. In Germany he was known as 'Himalayan Bauer', though by 1963 he had abandoned serious expeditionary climbing and devoted himself to writing and to encouraging the German climbing movement.

Paul Bauer arranged for me to have some climbing in the Bavarian Alps on the Austrian frontier, which was all rock work naturally, for there are no glaciers in those mountains, and I saw the young German climbers doing some very remarkable things. It was good to try myself out on rock again, for in the Himalaya, where all my climbing had been done until 1953, it was nearly all a matter of ice and snow, and the rock in any case is mostly not so good for climbing as in Europe. It was only when I went to Switzerland in 1954 that I really learnt to handle rock properly; now I have learnt quite a lot and am fairly competent, though when I am at home I still prefer ice and snow work because of the brittle and loose nature of Himalayan rock. My Italian friend Compagnoni told me once of the troubles he had had with loose rock on his ascent of K2 in the Karakoram, the world's second highest mountain, in 1954.

I have now climbed rock in many parts of Europe, in Switzerland on Dr Glatthard's course, in France in the Chamonix region with Lionel Terray, in Italy with Achille Compagnoni, and now in Germany and Austria also, apart from the rocks of our own training area in Sikkim.

11: AMERICAN ADVENTURES

The Indian Government in 1964 invited me to go to New York, where the World Fair had been organised for that year, to promote Darjeeling tea, and Daku was to go with me. There was sense in this, for not only was I a Darjeeling man but I am very fond of tea and I always carry a lot of it around with me on my travels to give to the people I visit. All mountaineers are fond of tea. I drink it in great quantities. In the mountains it is very good, for it is hot and thirst-quenching at the same time. Coffee does not quench a thirst; it only makes you more thirsty and for climbing people that is no good at all. We use a lot of tea at our Institute, both at headquarters and in the field, and when there are guests at my home in Darjeeling, tea is the first thing I offer them. When we went to Everest in 1953 Ang Lahmu sent six pounds of tea up to us from Darjeeling and we used it all. In the Himalaya there is really only one other drink and that is chang or rice beer, which can be found in all the little villages, where they make it themselves. In 1953 a photograph was taken at South Col, at 26,000 feet, when Ed Hillary and I arrived back from the summit and were given tea to revive us. This photograph was later used as an advertisement for the Darjeeling brand.

So at the New York fair I made propaganda for tea and it seems to have been successful. The Indian Government was very appreciative. I made some appearances on television and I spoke on sound radio too, and I was often report- ed in the newspapers. I was very busy for three weeksand we gave samples away to all sorts of important people, and while we were there we were introduced to more persons than I can remember the names. Among them were U Thant, the Secretary-General of United Nations at that time, and the Governor of New York, and there was a grand reception to welcome us to the city. It was my first visit to America and in most ways I enjoyed it, but I found the bustle and the noise too much. It was all too big and everyone seemed in a hurry. I am not really a city man. I remember that once, when I looked up to see the top of one of the tall buildings, I leaned back so far that my hat fell off; on another occasion they took me to the top of the Empire State building to look down on the city below, but somehow it seemed very different from looking down from the top of a mountain—everything looked quite remote. Among other places we visited was the Zoo, where to my surprise we found two yaks that reminded me keenly of the days long ago when as a boy I looked after them on the mountainsides. When I spoke to the two yaks in the Tibetan language they actually turned towards me with an eager look.

I visited the American Alpine Club, of which I had been made a member, and there I met American climbing friends who had been out to Everest the year before, including Jim Whitaker (he had reached the summit with my nephew

Gombu), as well as Luther (Lute) Jerstad, Tom Hornbein, Willi Unsoeld, Barry Bishop and others. Some of these climbers then invited Daku and me to join them in a climb of Mount Rainier, which is in the Cascade Mountains in the western state of Washington and one of the highest mountains in the United States. It would be a particularly interesting trip since all of us except Daku had at one time or another been on the summit of Everest. As for Daku, she had made up her mind to go on a climb even though her mountaineering experience so far was limited to Sikkim, where she had been with me on occasions. This American journey was in fact her first ever away from the Himalayan world in which she had been born.

So to the Cascades we went and the ascent of Mount Rainier was eventually done by moonlight, starting at midnight. We were divided into two ropes: Lute led one, with Daku in the middle and myself at the end, and Tom and Jim were together on the other. We followed a route up an ice-fall which, I was told, had been done only twice before. It was called the Nisqually Ice-fall route and is usually considered difficult, but in that summer of 1964 many of the walls had already collapsed and technically there was really little serious work to be done. The lower part can be dangerous because of ice avalanches, but our luck was good and we made quite fast progress. All the same I found the climb quite serious enough; especially as I was not used to the American way of climbing with a very long rope between each climber, sometimes as long as a hundred feet. I prefer to climb my own way, on a short rope, and to do proper step-cutting in the Swiss fashion. But this was a bit slow for my American friends and all the time they were urging me on, calling to me: 'Come on, Tenzing, come on!' However, I stuck to the way I know best, as far as my friends would allow me.

Daku did very well, especially so since this was her first really serious climb. She was in great form, full of enthusiasm and enjoying herself. According to Lute, instead of keeping the rope taut at full stretch, she was moving up close behind him all the time. At times, he said, he found this quite unnerving. But in fact she only wanted to talk to him! She could speak only a little English at that time and Lute could speak only a little Nepali. Yet they managed to make themselves understood.

The weather on this climb was good. It was midsummer. The moon was very bright and the night was quiet. In the ice-fall, when we were cutting steps, the blows of the axe and the sound of the falling pieces of ice was like music. Daku said that she felt as if someone close by was playing on some strange musical instrument. There was no need for any light but that of the moon, not even flashlights, and when we got to the top at about nine in the morning the sun had been up for hours. By then it had become hazy and the view, which must be very grand when clear, was poor, though to the south we could make out two other great mountains, Mount Adams and Mount Hood.

I was rather disappointed in the summit. Instead of being a real peak, like the summits I have known in the Alps and Himalaya, it turned out to be a big hollow basin which, when we were there, was partly filled with snow. The basin is a good distance across and quite deep. I now know that it is, of course, a dead volcano and there are three separate summits on the rim of the old crater. Many of the mountains in this part of America are similar in shape to Rainier; they, too, are old volcanoes, standing out quite isolated from one another, their steep sides rising sharply from the surrounding land and their upper slopes covered with snow. Mount Hood, in Oregon, which we were to climb on a later trip, was in this way very similar to Rainier. Daku was the very first woman to ascend Mount Rainier by the south-west route, a really remarkable achievement.

After the climb we all went down to the inn—the Paradise Inn—from which most of the climbs begin. I was very thirsty and I drank about half a dozen beers one after the other. I thought I was drunk after that, but I was still very thirsty and wanted another. Somehow I managed not to drink more. Years after, in 1972, I climbed with Lute in these mountains again, but in the meantime there were other adventures in the American mountains with him and our friends. Lute is a very good friend and a great companion in the mountains. He is also a great teacher of mountaineering and has been most successful with experiments in teaching mental patients to climb, helping by doing so to relieve them of their troubles. By communing with nature they seem to improve, and the actual business of rock-climbing seems to remove their tensions. I have not seen any of this at work, but at the Trento film festival Lute gave a talk with films about his work in this direction.

Jim Whitaker I am very fond of too: a fine mountaineer, a real gentleman and most hospitable. He lent equipment to Daku and myself on our American climbs. To me he seems himself like a big mountain. As a result of the Rainier climb Daku became very keen on the sport and eager to do more. Meanwhile we returned to Darjeeling, stopping on the way only to look at the Niagara Falls.

Two weeks after our return we were told by the Indian Government that our work in New York had been most successful and that in return they would like to do something for my family. I asked them what it was they had in mind and they said, your daughter Nima is very well educated and we would like to employ her at the Tea Board. So she joined them and for the next five years she was abroad and travelled in many parts of the world—Britain, France, Italy, Germany, Austria, Scandinavia, Switzerland—many places, working on tea promotion. It was a long and continuous tour.

A few years after the New York trip, in 1968, the Scandinavian air lines, SAS, opened a new jet service between Bangkok and Copenhagen by way of Tashkent, and they invited me, as one of a hundred guests, mostly from the Far East, to join the trip. And so from Bangkok (first of all I had to get there from

Darjeeling) we flew right across the roof of Asia, seeing many famous high mountains on the way. I spent the two following weeks in Scandinavia and saw many parts of all three countries, and paid a visit to the Norwegian Alpine Club, where a reception had been organised for us. We met the King of Denmark and members of his family, and in Copenhagen I saw again Prince Peter of Greece, whom I had already known for a long time, having first met him in Kalimpong and Darjeeling. He can speak Tibetan, and does so extremely well.

In Norway we met the Norwegian climber who had made the first successful ascent of Tirich Mir in 1950, the highest point of the Hindu Kush. This was especially interesting for me because, many years earlier, in 1939 to be precise, I had gone with a British lady climber and her husband on an attempt on this same big and beautiful mountain, but we had failed. The weather had forced us back when we were at about 23,000 feet. Actually we were too small an expedition for so serious a climb and our strength and equipment were not really enough. It is not a difficult mountain, and with more men and equipment we might well have succeeded, but anyway it was not intended as a really serious expedition and Mr and Mrs Smeeton were in the mountains mainly for fun. So nobody was worried or unhappy about our failure. The Norwegian mountaineer showed us his film and the slides of his expedition and these brought back a vivid memory of an early adventure, especially as Tirich Mir, being on the borders of Afghanistan, was the farthest I had ever been from Darjeeling until quite recent times.

Remembering that Norway is famous for its woollens I went to a shop with the object of buying a pullover. The shopkeeper asked me if l knew Tenzing and I answered that indeed I did know him. And then I asked him the reason for his question, and he replied that it was because I looked so much like Tenzing. Then I told him the truth, though he found it hard to believe because I was so far from home. And when I explained that I had come to his shop to buy a Norwegian pullover he insisted on presenting me with one.

My daughter Nima was working in Belgium at the time of this trip and she came up all the way to Copenhagen to be with me. She joined my trip and we enjoyed many excursions together during that fortnight. She was, of course, still working on tea promotion, but in Copenhagen she met a man whom she later married, a Filipino working as art director of *Asia Magazine*. His name is Noley Kelang. They have now been married for some years and after living for a while in Hong Kong and Singapore they have settled down in Manila with their baby son. So now I am a grandfather and the father-in-law of a Filipino. Pem-Pem, on the other hand, has three children, so I have four grandchildren in all.

12: RETURN TO BASE CAMP; A JOURNEY INTO BHUTAN

The years 1963 and 1964 had been especially notable for the travel they involved, and for a few years afterwards I was completely taken up with my work at the Institute, preparing students at headquarters and training them in the mountains, and in between, when I was free, looking after my own home and family. The one journey of any importance which I took in this period was to Burma on an official visit. The Principal of HMI and myself had been invited there by Colonel Wang, chairman of the Burmese Mountaineering Association, who had in fact done the basic course in Darjeeling. Subsequently he took a great interest in rock climbing and in trekking, for there are no mountains for climbing in Burma and unless people can get to India for the sport they have to make do with the rock scrambles their own country affords. I had to talk on these subjects to the boys and girls of Burma and give the authorities what guidance I could in their wish to take up the sport of climbing.

The Burmese gave us the warmest of welcomes and we saw enough of Burma to know that it is indeed a very beautiful place, visiting many pagodas and temples, and on one occasion coming upon a Gurkha village which had the curious effect of making me think I was back in Nepal.

Then in 1969 Pem-Pem and I were invited to take part in the Rencontre Hautes Montagnes which was to take place in Zermatt at the end of August. The invitation came from the president of the Ladies Alpine Club, Baroness von Reznicek. But first we were taken to Engelberg and spent three days skiing on Titlis and sightseeing. Then we moved on to Murren to meet Dr Feuz, to lunch with him and the Japanese Ambassador and six young Japanese climbers (including one girl) who had recently climbed the Eiger north face, which I could see from Murren. They were certainly an enthusiastic, strong and youthful group and to meet them was a great pleasure to both of us. Eventually, after a visit to Raymond Lambert and a dinner party with members of the Swiss Everest expeditions in Geneva, and a further meeting with Dr Feuz and Carl Weber in Zurich, and a happy meeting with Albert Eggler in Bern, we arrived in Zermatt for the meet. It lasted a week; sixty members of the Rencontre attended and fifteen nations were represented.

I had never been to Zermatt before and we were fascinated by its great natural beauties, especially by the sight of the Matterhorn from the side by which it is best known. I had only seen the mountain before from the Italian side and from the Plateau Rosa when skiing with Compagnoni. The people of Zermatt gave us a great welcome. There were parties at the great hotels and excursions, and when it was all over we left for Meiringen and Rosenlaui to visit Dr Glatthard fifteen years after the training course which he had given me before our Institute got started.

While in Zermatt I met again my old friend Mrs Sutter, which took me back more than twenty years to my first climbs after the war and especially to my work with the Swiss expedition which came out in 1947 to climb a number of virgin peaks in northern India and on the Tibetan frontier. Mrs Sutter—then Mrs Annelies Lobner—was a member of the party; Rene Dittert, with whom I was on Everest later, was another, and so was Andre Roch. This was the expedition during which Wangdi Norbu, the head Sherpa, fell a thousand feet with Mr Sutter, to whom he had been roped, but both survived. Mr Sutter was only shaken and bruised, but Wangdi had a broken leg as well as severe cuts from Sutter's crampon points, and during the night that followed he tried to commit suicide because he thought he had been abandoned. He had in fact been made comfortable in an emergency tent until further help could be brought in the morning. However, we got him down from the mountain and he lived, but he was never the same again. When he had gone I had been appointed Sirdar in his place, which was the reali-sation of a Sherpa's ambition, though saddened by the misfortune of a friend.

I had enjoyed this expedition with the Swiss. For the first time on an expedition I felt on equal terms with my employers; indeed I felt towards them not as Sherpa to Sahibs, but rather as friends. There was the beginning of a romance during this trip, for Mrs Lohner later married Mr Sutter and it was to their home that I went after my visit to Rosenlaui.

In Mr Sutter's factory he has quite a number of Tibetan workers, refugees who had fled before the Chinese armies and had been brought to Switzerland for refuge. The Swiss have taken a great interest in Tibetans, have given them work and are educating their children. We visited one of these colonies, which has its own Buddhist monastery, and we dined with the Tibetans on their own typical food.

In November that same year my good friend Lute Jerstad of the American Everest expedition of 1963, with whom Daku and I had climbed Mount Rainier in Washington State five years earlier, invited us—Daku, my son Norbu, and myself—to join him and a group of Americans on a trek from Kathmandu to the Everest base camp by way of Solu Khumbu. It was a private group, just friends of Lute's, about fourteen of them, people he had guided on climbs through the years, and friends of friends, and one of these had asked him if there was anyone he would especially like to join the trip, someone who might make it even more interesting to the group. That is how we came to be there, on a trip which was for me especially interesting since I had not been back to these mountains for ten years; as a result I spent rather a lot of time getting to know my many relatives again after such a long interval. Barry Bishop of the 1963 expedition was one of the party too, and we were twenty-seven persons in all, including Sherpas and porters, Norbu being by far the youngest of the party, celebrating his seventh birthday at base camp.

From Kathmandu to Base is 175 miles and the route goes up and down all the way, crossing many high passes and plunging down thousands of feet again in the valleys between. Famous expeditions had passed this way, the two Swiss parties of 1952 and the British 1953 expedition amongst them. It was then a little-known route, except to the people of the region; few Europeans or Americans knew anything about it until after the Second World War, for Nepal had been a closed land, and only when Tilman and Shipton were searching for the southern approach to Everest did these trails open up. But when we joined Lute's trek nearly twenty more years had passed and people were using the route in greatly increasing numbers, though an air-strip at Lukla in Khumbu has already made the long early part of the journey unnecessary, leaving them only four or five days from airstrip to the valley head. I think this is a pity because it is a beautiful and interesting journey, over high grasslands and through deep forests of enormous trees, with giant rhododendrons and magnolias which at the right season can make the land unbelievably colourful.

It took us sixteen days to reach Base Camp, having travelled a short way at the beginning by taxi and then taken a two day rest. So actual walking time was fourteen days and we got to our destination on 8 December. In Solu Khumbu, at every house we went to, in every village we passed through, people came out to greet me, people who had not seen me for many years but had not forgotten. Each time they would invite us in, Lute and me, for chang and rakshi, and quite often we would not get into camp until very late in the evening because we had been so busy drinking with my friends along the way.

It was good to see Everest again and to show it to Norbu and to answer his many questions about the mountain and its first ascent. For him the journey from Kathmandu had been no trouble at all; he had enjoyed every day and he was always running along ahead of us all. But everything in the Everest scene had greatly changed. The glacier where we had set up the first camp in 1952, the Swiss camp, and where the British camp was pitched the next year, was unrecognisable. In 1953 it had been difficult to erect the tents on the moraine, which was full of ice. But since then the glaciers had been steadily moving back and the ice in 1969 was three miles farther up the valley. At the site of the camp, where in 1952 and 1953 there had been a great deal of pinnacle ice, there was now no ice at all. All was gone; only the moraine remained. And the same sort of change had taken place on the route from Base Camp to Camp I, where there was still some ice, though it was vanishing fast. The Khumbu icefall was badly wasted and had broken up, and I thought that it would be even more difficult to work through than when we had done so sixteen years before. Being shorter, it was that much steeper: the same height had to be covered in a shorter distance and over much rougher going. None of us attempted to enter it, but I could see that it would be very difficult, very dangerous, to try to camp in it, and that anyone who wanted to reach the Western Cwm would have to force a way through in a single day from the foot of the fall. Quite a few bridges would be needed too.

The ice had retreated everywhere and all the glaciers had sunk away. At first I was very puzzled. I could recognise very little and all my familiar landmarks were gone. Down the valley from the Base Camp there had been a tributary glacier descending from the region of Pumori to join the main stream of ice. But this ice which it had joined, and the side glacier itself, had vanished and the surface had sunk so low that from a point on it where it had once been possible to look clearly at Everest, that mountain could no longer be seen, no part of it at all. Maybe the surface had sunk as much as a thousand feet. Nothing, anyway, looked as I remembered it, and I even began to think that maybe my memory had played me a trick. But then I thought suddenly of the photographs that my two daughters had taken on their visit to Base Camp in 1955, fourteen years earlier, including one from the very point on the Chakri Glacier where I was then standing so puzzled. So when I got home I asked to see those pictures and they proved quite certainly that from the point on the glacier where you could clearly see Everest in 1955 you could no longer do so in 1969. The whole scene had changed; so much rock and debris where ice had been, and all the levels lowered.

The simple reason for this change is, I think, that for many years much less snow has fallen in the mountains in winter and during the monsoons, and the summers have been hot and dry. In Darjeeling until 1954 there had always been snow in winter, but since then the snow has not come. And everywhere in the Himalaya it is the same. The monsoon is not what it was; the lack of rain lower down has been bad for the farmers, while in the mountains it no longer snows so much, though the winds are very strong. It has happened in Sikkim too, especially in the Kangchenjunga region, where sometimes there has been no snow at all, while the summers have been scorching. Our old people say that the farther people go up into the mountains the warmer the weather will become. Certainly, since the ascent of Everest the climate of the Himalaya has changed very noticeably.

There have been other changes too and in a way more serious. The weather can change and the snows will return. But when people change they seldom go back to their old ways. In the whole Khumbu region the roads have been greatly improved and the valley is wide open to the world. The people there have all now been influenced by modern civilisation and of course the standard of living has risen. All of which is good in a way; on the other hand many people have gone away, especially the younger ones. Until the ascent of Everest most of the Khumbu people had for centuries been content to live in the villages and cultivate the land, and except for those like me who moved away to Darjeeling they never saw anything of the outside world. I shall have more to say about this later, but one thing is sure, we cannot turn back the clock and the most important thing is probably to make the conditions which will bring the young people back to stay. Meanwhile, in the upper valley in 1969 a great deal of what I remembered of Sherpa life had already gone; the tourists were already seeing to that.

Many visitors, on their way in large groups to visit Base Camp, stop to look at the old and famous monastery of Thyangboche, one of the highest in the world and until twenty-five years ago almost unknown to the outside world. A smaller version of the great Rongbuk monastery in Tibet, where many of the older Everest expeditions passed, Thyangboche was a centre of Tibetan Buddhist faith and culture to which the whole region turned. It was a flourishing community when the first exploratory expeditions to Everest through Nepal arrived. It stands upon a wooded and grassy saddle above the point where the Imya Khola and the Dudh Kosi rivers meet, overlooked by many giant summits, including Ama Dablan and Kangtenga, though Everest itself is scarcely visible from the monastery, only its summit and the white plume of blown snow.

Today the monastery has very few monks. Once very beautiful, the place has now become quite dirty, due mainly to the visiting tourists, and it is falling into disrepair. When I met the head lama I was saddened when he told me that no one today wants to become a lama. I asked why this was and he replied that there are so many tourists and that all the young men and boys want to go with them as porters. Also that after Hillary's school had opened, everyone wanted to go there and get a western-style education instead of the Tibetan teaching the lamas had given them in years gone by. And if they no longer learn to read Tibetan then the culture that has for so long been centred upon Thyangboche will vanish too and the monastery will be deserted because there will be no monks to keep it going. So, although I have much praise for Hillary's school, in the end it is certain to destroy the traditional Sherpa way of life, at least as I know it. It will continue so long as the old people remain alive, but no longer. Once educated in the western way, the boys want to move off to Kathmandu or elsewhere in Nepal and they are quickly swallowed up in the general population and the past is soon forgotten.

I visited the new hospital too, for the first time; it is doing wonderful work.

On that trek in 1969 I did no climbing. I looked after Norbu, who was too young for anything but trekking. But Daku, Lute and another American climbed a mountain of about 19,000 feet very close to Pumori; it was Daku's highest mountain so far. The weather throughout the trek was wonderful and the mountains around Everest were splendid to look on. We stayed at base camp for three days.

When we had passed through the village of Kunde on the way up, Lute had left word that on our return he would buy all the beer for a party to bring all my old friends and his together. So on the way back four barrels of chang awaited him. Everyone gathered in the house of Mingma Tsering, who had in fact been with Lute on Everest in 1963, in the upstairs room—about 120 or 150 people at any one time—drank, danced and sang until the early hours of the morning. And when it was all over many were very tipsy and could hardly find their way down the stairs. The next morning they were supposed to be on the march by seven, but few got out of their sleeping bags before nine or ten, and all, Sherpas included, had large hangovers.

I should add that while this party was going on, Daku and I had stolen away to visit relatives in Namche Bazar, so we were saved the bad heads of the next morning.

The Lukla air-strip is only a three-day march from Base Camp and the flight to Kathmandu took thirty-five minutes. When I remembered the long marches of 1952 and 1953, and the toilsome ascents and descents of the ridges, I felt in the aeroplane as if I were dreaming.

The beautiful Himalayan state of Bhutan lies to the east of Sikkim and in recent times it has been even more difficult to enter. Only with the permission of the King was it possible to do so and this was not often given. The number of people who have been able to travel freely—especially climbers—is very small indeed. Therefore its wonderful mountain ranges and the beautiful but remote northern parts of the land are still very difficult to reach and penetrate and are little known to outsiders. Long ago one or two travellers and climbers came over from Tibet, which was itself open at that time, but not since then. A number of British climbers were allowed in a few years ago and some Swiss travellers too: Dr Gansser, who travelled through the remote and lovely region known as Lunana, up among the mountains in the north; also his daughter who, with Blanche Olschak of Zurich, travelled extensively among the monasteries and recorded many of the beautiful things they contain. Political troubles have kept Bhutan a comparatively closed land until very recently, but it is closed no longer.

Bhutan is very much larger than Sikkim. Its people are almost entirely Bhutias, a tribe of Tibetan origin and speaking a form of Tibetan too. They came over the eastern passes many centuries ago. One difference from Sikkim is that there are so few people of Nepalese origin, whereas in Sikkim by far the majority are Nepali. In Bhutan less than five per cent. The Bhutias are a very religious people and the huge mountains, covered with snow and ice, that glitter against the deep Himalayan skies, forming the frontier with Tibet, have protected their beliefs against change. Now that a certain amount of travel has been allowed and roads are being built I wonder how long these traditional beliefs and way of life will last. They did not last long in Nepal, once the gates were opened, and we know the consequences. At present there is no accommodation for tourists in Bhutan, but people will come with tents, carrying their provisions, as happened in Nepal. Although the people are not poor, left to themselves, they have nothing to spare for a tourist invasion; but as in Nepal they would be too polite, too naturally hospitable, to refuse to provide food and drink, and then there will be trouble again, for the people will go short themselves. At present Bhutan is still the most remote and least changed mountain land in the world. I would like to think it will stay that way, but I am not an optimist. Change will come with the tourists and they are already arriving.

In Bhutan there are many extraordinary fortress monasteries known as dzongs and there is nothing like them anywhere else in the world, not even in the Himalaya; some of them I visited with a Swiss party which I led in 1970. It was a mixed group of men and women, some of them—in particular Rene Dittert and Gabriel Chevalier—being old climbing friends from the 1952 expeditions. Daku came with me and my youngest daughter too. We were twelve in all. I was able to take this party in because, despite restrictions still in force, for this was six years ago, I was already well known to the King and his approval had been given. Bhutias being of Tibetan origin like the Sherpas, we speak more or less the same language. The King takes an interest in mountaineering and has actually sent some Bhutias to learn the sport at our Institute in Darjeeling. He was very good to my party and he invited Daku, Diki and myself to tea.

This was not a climbing expedition, but some strenuous walking was involved. We toured some of the more easily reachable parts of the country and visited some of the wonderful monastery buildings, especially the 'Tiger's Cave' at Taktshang, where the temple buildings seem to hang on the sheer rock face, one on top of the other, reached by people with steady heads up an extraordinary combination of steep steps in the rock wall and precarious wooden ladders. There are hermit cells there as well, clinging to the rock like the nests of birds or wasps and reachable only by very dangerous ladder systems. The Tiger's Cave—or Tiger's Den- Monastery is well over a thousand years old. Tigers actually did roam there once and the hermits, having purified the area, built their precarious cells as protection. More recently a new monastery has been built on the ridge opposite the Tiger's Cave, with a broad and easy road down the valley.

We saw the great Punakha Dzong too, a monastery fortress built where the 'Father and Mother' rivers meet, the Mo Chu and the Pho Chu; it is the royal winter residence, and reached from Thimphu, the capital, by a pass known as the Dochu La, from which the whole crescent-shaped northern frontier is seen, reaching from Chomolhari in the west to Zhagthi Kang in the east, with Tsering Kang (meaning 'The Glacier of Long Life'), Kankgkar Punsum ('The White Glacier of the Three Holy Brothers') and Masa Kang in between. This great mountain barrier is Bhutan's northern defence, for there are very few passes that can be used; only in the far east and the far west of the country are the passes really accessible. The view from Dochu La is quite unforgettable.

Punakha Dzong is reached by an old iron chain suspension bridge which swings and sways above the river. Its walls are of plaited bamboo and there are foot boards which make it safe enough. In the dzong are eighteen temples and wonderful treasures.

Another fortress we visited was the Wangdiphodang. It is said that its founder once saw a boy playing by the river and building a miniature dzong of pebbles. This the founder took to be an omen and it was at that spot that he built the fortress of which he had been dreaming for a long time. The boy's name was Wangdi, and the fortress was named after him.

There are magnificent mountains still to be climbed on Bhutan's northern frontier. Chomolhari ('Queen-Goddess of the Holy Mountains') was climbed by an Englishman, Spencer Chapman, and his Sherpa companion nearly forty years ago, but from the Tibetan side. Most of the rest must still be unclimbed, and in a way I hope they will remain so. The mountains of Bhutan are very sacred to the people, as their names show.

Five years after that trip with the Swiss, in 1975, I took a party of Americans into Bhutan at the end of a trip that had already included Nepal and Sikkim. This one itself was a sign of increasing tourism during the last few years, for it had been organised by a mountain travel agency in Kathmandu that had asked me to be its sirdar.

There are now no real difficulties about touring or trekking in Bhutan and the land is certain to become a new attraction for Western visitors, with great opportunities for adventure and mountaineering, or for people with a simple love of mountains. I only hope it will not be spoiled as other areas have been.

In 1971 I made my first journey to Japan at the invitation of the Japanese Alpine Club. This was not in any way a special celebration. Naturally we discussed mountaineering topics, for the Japanese are enthusiastic and successful climbers and have brought a number of expeditions to the Himalaya in recent years, including all-women parties, to attack most of the famous mountains—including the first attempt on the south-west face of Everest, recently conquered by Chris Bonnington's expedition. Anyway, when in Japan the Japanese climbers asked me for a certain amount of advice, especially concerning Sherpas and equipment, but this was not really the point of the trip, which was purely friendly. It was a short trip too. They took me to see many places and they gave me a week's skiing holiday at Saporo; this was in the year previous to the Olympic winter games and a great deal of building was going on in preparation. It was February and very cold, but there was plenty of snow and the skiing was excellent.

Since then I have been to Japan again, in 1976, this time on an official trip on behalf of Air India to promote Darjeeling among Japanese tour operators. We continued the trip to Manila and Hong Kong for the same purpose, but while in Japan I had an opportunity to meet many Japanese climbers, most of whom had been members of the Japanese Mount Everest Expedition. Daku came with me this time.

13. AGAIN AMERICA; NEW ZEALAND TOUR

Two years after the trek to Everest base camp with Lute Jerstad and his friends, and seven years after my first visit to the United States, we were back in the American West in 1971 at the invitation of Lute and his climbing friends. The Institute had given me special leave of absence and we were Lute's guests for a long stay that summer, when we spent a lot of time at his climbing school, talked about Everest and HMI to many audiences and visited some of the high mountain areas. It was a useful and enjoyable time, but also a bit exhausting, since I had engagements in Canada and New Zealand also.

In the West I gave about twenty talks in all, and during one of them, at the Explorers' Club in Los Angeles, I shared the evening with the astronaut Bill Anders, and our talks appeared to be most successful. Although I have now given so many in so many parts of the world to all sorts of audiences, I still do not enjoy public speaking and I do not believe I ever will. In Los Angeles I spoke also at a special gathering at the University of California, to which the general public was invited. It was a big occasion and included a screening of the film of the British ascent of Everest; even nearly twenty years after the climb there were cheers from the audience when the summit scene was shown and at the end of the film they all stood up to applaud. The audience, however, was a typically middle-aged one, as most of them are now except of course at schools, because few people of less than middle age can remember the climb at all. Most of the people at a university now were not even born when it took place. It was in Los Angeles that they made me an honorary citizen of the municipality.

The rest of the talks were mostly in connection with Lute's mountain adventure enterprise in Portland, Oregon. I spent a lot of time with him that summer and with his friend and business manager, Stan Armington, who also worked at that time as a guide. He dislikes making public appearances too. And with Jack Walston, another of Lute's colleagues, I went to Yosemite several times. I did no climbing in the Park, only walking, but it is a wonderful climbing area and I saw where the great climbs had been done that started what was almost a new kind of mountaineering with the extraordinary ascent of the huge vertical faces of El Capitan and Half Dome amongst many other rock walls. The mountains of Yosemite National Park are most beautiful, as in fact the whole region is, with great forests and wonderful giant trees—the redwoods so big that they make even the great fir trees look small and slender; some of them are over 3,000 years old—and lovely waterfalls. Thousands and thousands of people visit the Park every summer and use the campsites on the valley bottom, cooking their meals on the open fire-grates put there by the authorities. But they never seem to overcrowd the Park, nor to spoil it; it seemed to me to be unusually clean and free of rubbish in a way that really impressed me. And once you get away from the campsites and up into the mountains very few tourists are to be seen; they seem to stay close to their cars. Under intensely blue skies and amongst the great mountains and forests the peace and silence were wonderful. There are bears there, of course, that come around the campgrounds, especially at night, searching for food, but they do no one any harm if treated with respect.

Lute Jerstad is a man with many activities. I have mentioned already his work with mental cases. He also organises adventure camps and trekking holidays for children and young people which are very popular. He organises and personally leads treks in the Himalaya through the business he founded, Lute Jerstad Adventures, and he has a school of mountaineering on Mount Hood. This mountain is over 11,000 feet high, like Mount Rainier an old volcano with heavy snow cover on its upper slopes, about sixty-five miles east of Portland and a long way due south of Mount Rainier. At his school, Lute and his colleagues train Outward Bound instructors, youth leaders and people going on far-distant mountaineering expeditions. There are ice-climbing courses of all grades of difficulty, and special mountain rescue and medical courses. It is open every summer for about three months and it was especially interesting to me because of the comparison I could make with the work at HMI. So I took part in the various courses, and Daku actually completed her training as a climber on Mount Hood. Some time later she received from America her certificate for the courses she followed: a five-day ice-climbing seminar and a five-day mountain medicine and rescue course. The full climbing course lasts two weeks and it is basically much like any other mountaineering course. All students have to carry their own equipment everywhere, and though I cannot say that I learned anything really new, it was a useful experience.

We went to the Anthony Lakes 'adventure camp' too, where we went back-packing in the wilderness with the children, during which they learn to appreciate the land they trek through, its trees, flowers, rocks and scenery, and they really enjoy every moment.

Mount Hood is close to the Columbia river and its very impressive gorge. Like many mountains in north-west America it is very isolated and has a great deal of wind. Even in summer the weather can be quite severe and the glaciers are big because of the heavy snowfall and low temperatures. Mountaineering students there are likely to find all the extreme conditions they might meet on much higher mountain ranges in other parts of the world.

This I discovered for myself when I was out on the mountain with some of Lute's students who were taking instruction in ice-climbing techniques. It was about noon one day and, although the air until then had been quite calm, suddenly the wind began to blow very strongly and we decided at once to return to camp. But when we got to the site of the camp it was not there; everything had vanished, including the tents, carried off by the wind. Never before had I experienced anything like it, and I can claim to know—especially on Everest—what wind can do. Daku was with me and on our way down, with evening coming on, the darkness became really intense, so that we could scarcely see one another in the gloom. Daku is very small and light and I became afraid that the wind might blow her away; so I tied her into the rope and that is how we got down. Dust was everywhere; we were covered in it. Even my ears were filled. We all looked terribly dirty as we reached the foot of the mountain, where there is a small restaurant, but there we could clean up.

We took a river trip after that. It was on the John Day river, beginning at a place called Service Creek, and in large rubber rafts – each for six or even twelve persons – we followed the fast, roaring waters between the river's high walls for five days down to Cottonwood, very close to where it joins the great Columbia river. I have never before in my life been in this sort of boat—nor in any boat at all except for the one in Singapore—and I cannot swim a stroke. But there were two instructors with us and we had been given lifejackets, so we were not as worried as we might have been. It was an extraordinary experience for me to travel on the water for five days continuously; Daku learnt a great deal about how to manage the boats on this sort of water, but I felt very much a beginner and I really did not like it much. The land we travelled through seemed to me to be very like Tibet, with its great gorges and roaring waters and wild rocky scenery, and once, when I caught sight of a few cows, as an animal lover I felt happy.

We had one other very enjoyable experience before we left Oregon and that was a trip with about eighty-five boys and girls from all parts of the United States, with trekking, rock-climbing and boating, and survival tests as well. Daku took part with me and I can say we never enjoyed ourselves more. When the time came to break up the boys and girls began to cry and the sound of their weeping was almost like the sound of music, like singing. Many of them still remember us and write to us about the trek we shared with them.

In the end we could not make the journey to Mount Logan in the Yukon; it would have been a long one anyway and time was running short. So from Oregon we passed into Canada, having been invited there by Mr Trudeau, the Prime Minister. I had met him in Delhi at a big banquet given by Mrs Gandhi: he is a good skier and very interested in mountaineering. Now we met him and his wife in Calgary in time for the famous Stampede, which was one of the strangest and craziest things I have ever seen, with horse -and steer-riding of the maddest kind, exciting and very dangerous. While we were there two riders were killed taking part in these events.

The Canadian Alpine Club, which had organised our trip to Canada, had planned to show me some rock-climbing in the Rocky Mountains, but I had no time to take any proper part. Instead, I was shown the rock-climbs by helicopter and I came away feeling a bit embarrassed. I also met the two climbers, husband and wife, with whom I had climbed on Tirich Mir in the Hindu Kush in 1939: Mr and Mrs Smeeton. To see them again in their own country after over thirty years was indeed a real pleasure.

Now it was time to move on to New Zealand, where we had been invited by Sir Edmund Hillary, my comrade of the first ascent of Everest, and by the Himalayan Trust, which he had founded in order to build and maintain schools and hospitals in Sherpa areas, and also to do social work thereof other kinds. Funds were needed to continue and expand the work, so Ed Hillary wanted me to take part in a fundraising tour, at which we would show our film and interest people in what the Trust was doing. It was the first time I had been to New Zealand and he was anxious also to show me what a beautiful country it was. The tour lasted for nearly three weeks and although we did a lot of effective fundraising we saw a lot of the city and country life in between public performances, talking to schools and colleges and factories, and meeting the press.

Fortunately, I was not expected to give the speeches, but just to be present and appear on the stage when the film was shown. Ed did all the talking, but his speeches were short. I do not like public speaking and was glad not to have to do any. Often I have been involved in occasions which I have not really understood and in which I have had very little interest, just because of my story, and these occasions make me restless and depressed. But the New Zealand meetings were something different, and I had many opportunities for conversation with interesting people whose own interest in the Himalaya was genuine and understanding.

It was a strenuous trip; always on the move, we did a great deal in little time. In Auckland we were the guests of Sir Edmund and his wife, who has since died, with their daughter, in a terrible air accident. Their home, incidentally, was not at all like other New Zealand homes, but more like a Tibetan gompa. We were taken the very next day on a trip round the harbour of Waitemata in a yacht called *Young Nick*, whose skipper was Peter Mulgrew, one of Hillary's polar team of 1958, who three years later lost both legs in an attempt to climb Makalu in the Nepal Himalaya. Now with two metal legs he is a skilful sailor and a very witty man. This trip was followed by a party at the Hillary home to meet members of the Himalayan Trust, the Lions Club of Auckland, who are great supporters of the Trust, and the New Zealand Alpine Club. The next day we visited schools and colleges in the Auckland area as well as factories which were involved in making materials and articles that were used in Nepal, and there was a public fund-raising performance at the Embassy Theatre.

Next we passed on to Wellington, where we called upon the Prime Minister, Sir Keith Holyoake, also the Mayor, and we lunched with the Indian

High Commissioner. But one of the most memorable events of our New Zealand journey was a visit to the huge sheep lands of Mr H . E. Riddiford, a farmer and solicitor who had been on the Everest reconnaissance of 1951 and a Cho Oyu expedition a year later. Our journey took us afterwards to Christchurch, and there we were the guests of Norman Hardie and his wife; Norman, like Hillary, is an old campaigner in the Nepal Himalaya and is well known to the Sherpas of Solu Khumbu. In Christchurch we visited schools and factories, then enjoyed a jet-boat trip with Jon Hamilton in brilliant weather in the spectacular gorge of the Waimakariri river, and paid a visit to Michael Murchison's enormous mountain estate, on which there is a ski-field (when there is snow), and a lake with a hydro-electric station. It was a long drive from Christchurch and it was late winter, and to mountain people it was all looking most attractive. The hundreds of Aberdeen Angus beef cattle we saw had been trained to come to the feeding truck when a horn was blown. We drove into an apparently empty paddock, sounded the car horn and in no time at all we had a following of two hundred hungry cattle. Being winter still the spring growth of grass had not begun.

In the woolshed after lunch we saw sheep being shorn and I was amazed by the length and quality of the fleece. I have not had a lot to do with sheep, but such wool as that I had not seen before. Nor had Daku, who was greatly impressed. We saw the sheep dogs working as well.

These are some of the aspects of New Zealand life that I shall always remember: the size of the farms, the number and quality of the sheep and cattle, and the great sense of work without fuss. All this outdoor activity went on in the most impressively calm way, quietly but with great effect. Always, wherever we go in the world, what we like to see is the farming world, the cattle, the sheep, the dogs and horses, and in New Zealand it seemed to us that there was more of this going on than anywhere else we had seen so far.

Among other places we visited in Christchurch was the Ellis sleeping bag factory. The Ellis bags had been used on Everest in 1953 and on Kangchenjunga later, and other articles that were made there, like down jackets and mattresses, have been supplied to other Himalayan expeditions. The founder of the business was a member of Sir Edmund's polar party of 1958.

Dunedin was our next stop, with visits to schools, factories and the University, and then came a trip into the mountains of the Mount Cook area, staying at the famous Hermitage hotel, with a ski plane flight over the glaciers. There was no time, as usual, for any mountaineering, but I could see that these wonderful mountains, heavily covered with snow and ice, offered extraordinarily good sport.

We then drove to Wanaka. On the way a number of people came to meet us for a picnic beside the Ohau river; they were all people with experience of the Himalaya. The picnic place was in a broad valley, bare of forest but within view of many great mountains, quite close. Wanaka itself, where we spent the night, is a holiday resort with a big lake and a national park.

The helicopter flight the next day to the ski fields was a disappointment. Visibility was bad; warm rain was falling and only the children of the party put on their skis – the Hillary and Hardie children. Hardie, too, had been a mountaineer and had made some remarkable journeys in the Khumbu region before it became overrun, climbing with Hillary and others there in the year after Everest.

Queenstown was our last stop, a big and beautiful mountain village beside a big lake, with skiing and other mountain sports available, golf and fishing as well. I do not really like zoos and their captive animals, but I remember the one at Queenstown especially for its many varieties of deer. I was told that nearly all the kinds shown were not native to New Zealand but had been introduced to the country in fairly recent times, since when they have become a pest.

This had been a very successful trip, both for us and for the Trust. We always stayed, wherever we went, in the homes of people who had been on expeditions with Sherpas and we felt very much at home. Amongst the many people we met were Dr McKinnon and his wife; he had been the first doctor at Kunde hospital and spoke Sherpa extremely well.

We raised a worth-while amount of money—$14,000 – for the Sherpa schools and hospitals, and I ought to mention that the New Zealand doctors who take charge of the hospital at Kunde do so quite freely; they stay in Khumbu for a two-year term and they earn nothing. It is all a voluntary service and it is really marvellous work. These doctors make a major contribution to the health of the whole area. And my only complaint about the schools is that they have never had a Sherpa teacher to keep the Sherpa speech alive. There are now about fourteen Sherpa schools run by the Himalayan Trust, with about 600 children and a score or more of teachers.

But the Trust does a lot of other work in the region, like building, maintaining and repairing bridges, improving water supplies, and the schools are always in need of improvement and repair. So funds are always needed and Sir Edmund, who visits Khumbu every year and stays there for quite a while each time, is tireless in his search for money. During our tour cheques were presented by many schools and organisations, and factories presented their goods. Nevertheless, Sir Edmund insisted that fund-raising was not the only purpose of our visit, nor even the main one. It was also to show New Zealand to Daku and me, and we had been a long time coming. At the end he said he hoped that we would come again soon and perhaps climb Mount Cook.

Two days after our Queenstown stop we were on our way back to America, landing at Los Angeles, but stopping on the way to visit Nima, then living in Hong Kong. We stopped briefly at Honolulu too; it was now September and I found Hawaii unbearably hot.

We spent very little time in the United States on this return journey; it was mainly to talk to friends in San Diego who had planned that in 1972 I should go to South America, Africa and other parts of the world I had not yet seen. It was to be almost a world tour and last about five months, but after we got home we learned that the plan had fallen through largely from lack of funds, but also because in so many places there seemed to be military or political trouble of some kind.

By the time we stopped in San Diego we were already longing to be home and were missing our children very much. It had been a long journey and we were now tired. Also, I was becoming weary of American food in particular and western food generally and on several occasions I succeeded in persuading Stan Armington to take us to a Chinese restaurant where we could settle down to good Sherpa-sized plates of rice, much more to our liking. And it was already September and I had to think about my work at the Institute. For all this summer I had enjoyed special leave of absence; HMI does not close down when there is no climbing or teaching to be done and there are plenty of other activities to attend to.

So South America and Africa remain two places I have never seen and I think that possibly I may never see them. Yet I have been to so many parts of the world in the last twenty-three years, much more than most people ever do, certainly more than I ever dreamed of when I was a boy and herding the yaks on the pastures not far from Everest. I have seen many of the world's great cities - London, New York, Moscow, Geneva, Zurich, Rome, Delhi, Los Angeles, San Francisco, Sydney, Auckland, Copenhagen, Leningrad—many, many more—and I have seen the mountains of many lands. But I always gladly travel back to Darjeeling and the Himalayan snows and to Khumbu, where I was born and my ambitions first grew.

14: AFTER TWENTY YEARS

While in America I had been asked by Lute Jerstad to take part in an Everest trek that same autumn (1971). As it turned out, only four tourists signed for it, but it was run nevertheless. Lute organises these trips from Portland in Oregon, so the trekkers were all American. Stan Armington was leader and my daughter Pem-Pem joined us by flying into Lukla and continuing with the rest of us on foot to the base camp.

The entire trek covered 400 miles and we had sixty-five porters between us, for we carried from Kathmandu everything we needed to avoid attempting to live off the land, as so many parties, especially the unorganised ones, do to the detriment of the local people. For as the trekking season progresses meat and eggs, chickens and even vegetables get scarce everywhere and so do other supplies. This not only produces problems for the tourists themselves, but it brings real hardship to the peasants, even hunger at times. Some places, the ones close to Kathmandu, have plenty of food, but the mountain villages have little of their own except potatoes and eggs and a few chickens, and the rest has to be imported from lower down; nothing now comes over from Tibet as it used to years ago. Also, not so much food is being produced in valleys like the Khumbu because of partial depopulation. Yet Sherpas are incurably hospitable and never refuse a traveller food if there is anything available. This means that someone is going to have nothing to eat eventually, and that someone is of course the peasant.

Before the tourists came the people in the mountains usually had enough for themselves and were mostly self supporting, except when the crops failed. It was always a fairly marginal way of living, and when the crops did fail the peasants, especially in the highest areas, went hungry and starved, and some actually died of it. It was then no use for the people to go down to other villages for help; they themselves in those circumstances had little or nothing to give away. So the tourist who expects to buy food as he passes along has only worsened the problem, and until local production gets a lot better it is both wise and proper that visitors should bring everything necessary with them. If they bring too much they can always leave some of it behind.

On this trip with Stan to Base Camp and at the start of the return journey, while I was visiting relatives in the Khumbu, Pem-Pem and the whole party spent several days at Thyangboche and were lucky as well as privileged to see the Mani Rimdu, an annual festival at the monastery in which the lamas dance in fantastic costumes. Afterwards, descending the hill from the monastery, Pem-Pem slipped and fell, breaking a bone at the base of her spine. Friends rallied round and carried her to Lukla air-strip, a journey of some days, and from there she was flown to hospital in Kathmandu, where she soon recovered.

As on the journey two years earlier, I was in a rather odd situation. I was neither Sahib nor Sherpa. That is to say, I had no job to do, but on the other hand I was not exactly one of the tourists. This is why, probably, I spent so much time away from the party visiting relatives and friends in Khumbu. Nevertheless, while trekking we were all able to talk a lot between ourselves and I believe I was able to make the journey a bit more interesting for the visitors.

I was very impressed by one of the Sherpas in particular: Phorbu Geljen, who came from Pangum, a strong, capable and intelligent man. So I arranged for him to come to HMI at Darjeeling for a full course of training, which he did and made great progress. It was a very great blow to me and to all of us when he was killed the same year (1972) by an avalanche during the Korean expedition to Manaslu. This expedition was a total disaster, probably the worst disaster of its kind ever to take place in Nepal: five of the climbers and ten of the Sherpas died.

While I was in Khumbu I was able to do something that was and still is very close to my heart. I spoke of it quite early in this book and I expect I shall speak of it again. It is the question of the decline of Sherpa culture and the Tibetan language, partly as a result of not having any place in the education of the children in the Khumbu schools. Ever since Everest and the opening up of the valley this has worried me and I have also been worried by the complaint often made that I personally have done little or nothing for the Sherpa people to whom I belong. This, of course, is simply not true; at the Institute I help to train Sherpas year after year to play an important part in Indian mountaineering and they do get work as a result, either with expeditions or in the trekking business. I think I can say also that twenty years ago I helped to make the name of Sherpas famous throughout the world as a distinguished and trusty mountain people, and this brought a certain amount of employment to the community. What I have regretted are some of the social and cultural consequences and I have never ceased to say that something should be done about them. I do not want to see the true Sherpa life disappear, though I want to see the real standards of living rise and continue to rise. I had spoken of this to Stan and spent some time with him in Khumbu suggesting that they teach Tibetan again and do not neglect the local cultural traditions. Luckily we made it possible to employ a teacher at Jumbesi for a year to cover these subjects, and as a result there was a great celebration in the village. The old people were glad, because they really cannot understand the value of much of the modern teaching.

Then, in May 1972, exactly twenty years had passed since the first Swiss expedition to Everest, the first ever to attempt to climb the mountain from the south. There was a great reunion in Switzerland to celebrate the anniversary, and I was invited to attend by all the members of that expedition. In Geneva I saw a lot of my good friend Raymond Lambert, with whom I have kept in close touch ever since our great climb together, almost to the top, and I have stayed with him in Geneva on several occasions; so have some of my family. For me his house is almost a second home. I stayed in Switzerland altogether for three weeks, including celebrations in Rosenlaui as well as Geneva.

Ernst Feuz and Carl Weber of the Swiss Foundation for Alpine Research were at the celebrations and so were most of the original climbers. I like the Swiss, not merely because of the adventures I have shared with them or because of our close relations and all the help they gave us when setting up our Institute. Perhaps it is because theirs is, like Nepal, a small country and a mountain country, and I find them easy and friendly to live with. Carl Weber of Zurich, who did so much for Swiss climbing and skiing, has died since the 1972 reunion and I have personally lost a good and generous friend. The Foundation has given much help to mountaineers all over the world, technical help as well as financial; we in Darjeeling have benefited especially.

In Switzerland, which I had now been visiting at frequent intervals for twenty years, I found that the standard of living had risen higher and higher with each visit, but that the people had not changed at all as a result of their prosperity; they were still as hospitable, generous and unpretending as when I had first known them.

The Swiss reunion was a very enjoyable occasion and it was a very happy experience for me in particular to meet again so many of my former comrades. Air India made it possible for me to be there, as they did the trip that followed to Germany and Austria. This was not connected at all with mountaineering activity; it was a purely private visit, accompanying Commander Kohli, one of the best of Indian mountaineers, on a propaganda trip on behalf of the airline.

Another American trek in the Himalayas—this time in Sikkim—was laid on by an American agency for April 1973. Stan Armington was to lead it and I was to accompany the party. Stan came out to Darjeeling in December 1972 to discuss details and we talked a good deal about our separate
futures over a lot of Sikkim rum, for he then had some plan of setting himself up in Nepal as an independent trekking agent and leader. At the time of Stan's visit I had just returned from an HMI course in Sikkim on which I had been accompanied by my son Norbu. Norbu had celebrated his tenth birthday in Sikkim at 15,000 feet, just as three years earlier he had celebrated his seventh birthday at 16,000 feet in Nepal. On that earlier trek the whole party had signed his jacket; now it bore the signatures also of all the HMI staff on the training course. An impressive souvenir for any boy.

However, the April trek in Sikkim never came off.

The following year, 1973, after my duties with my students were ended, I visited

America again at the invitation of a man whom I had met during a tour organised by the Explorers' Club of New York—a tour, that is, in Nepal. He wanted me to come to Pennsylvania and talk to a gathering there, but I really did not understand what it was all about, only that I was expected to give my usual story of the ascent of Everest. I agreed to go, but when I got there I found that I was being used to promote a department store chain about which I knew nothing, and also a tour that was being organised to Tiger Tops, a jungle hotel in the southern forests of Nepal. Of course, my expenses were paid as well as my air fares, and I always enjoy travelling and meeting people, but this was not what I had expected. It was not the first time that such a thing has happened and I have become aware, when it is too late, that my appearance was all in aid of some other person's commercial interests, when I had thought they were really interested in Everest and mountaineering. Saddening lessons, but we have to put them down to experience.

This year marked the twentieth anniversary of the first ascent of Everest and an international meeting was arranged at Darjeeling to celebrate the occasion as well as the eighth anniversary of the great Indian ascent of 1965. The meeting began in the middle of May and lasted a week, and since it was organised by the Himalayan Mountaineering Institute a lot of the preparation fell to me and our instructors. There were thirty-seven foreign delegates and most of them were old friends of Everest days and very happy I was to see the mall together in my home town. Raymond Lambert was there with his wife, so were the other Swiss, Albert Eggler, Dr Wyss-Dunant, Dölf Reist, Jürg Marmet, Ernst Schmied as well as Norman Dyhrenfurth of the American expedition, and the French climbers of Annapurna represented by Gaston Rebuffat and Maurice Herzog, while the British were well represented by Lord Hunt, Charles Wylie, Bob Gregory and Chris Bonnington. Amongst the Indian representatives were Commander Kohli and Brigadier Gyan Singh.

They were a wonderful group of people to welcome to our Institute and we had a week-long seminar of films, lectures, discussions, excursions, dinners and entertainments of one kind and another. Amongst the films shown were Chris Bonnington's of the ascent—that time not quite successful—of the southwest face of Everest, Gaston Rebuffat's 'Between Heaven and Earth' and a French film of the ascent of Makalu. Lute Jerstad gave a talk in which we learnt of his work with mental patients already referred to. And at the Sherpa dinner-dance there was a sumptuous meal and much chang, with singing and dancing.

The trip to Tiger Hill, however, was a disappointment because of the thick mist that obscured any view whatever. I had been there so often in the past before the sun was up, or the clouds had formed, to look at the mountains in the dawn, with Everest so small and far away. The mountain was so much in the minds of our visitors that it was a great pity the sight was denied them.

Lord and Lady Hunt, with Colonel Wylie and Bob Gregory, arrived just as the meet was gathering, having completed a month-long celebration of their own in Nepal, with a stay of eight days in Khumbu, followed by a three-week trek across the hills to Darjeeling.

When the meet was over we set out for London again, having been invited by Lord Hunt to yet another anniversary celebration, this time in Wales, at Pen-y-Gwryd, in the shadow of Snowdon and many other mountains famous for their rock-climbs. So we—Daku and I—flew to Heathrow with Colonel Wylie on 22 May.

At the airport we were met by my old friend Colonel Alan Jenkins and his wife, whom I had not seen for nineteen years. Once they had lived in Katapahar, Darjeeling, where Gurkhas were once recruited for the British army. It was a happy meeting; the nineteen years seemed as nothing. Apart from the grey hairs the Colonel had acquired in the interval, it was as if we had parted only a few days before. So we drove to his home in the country where the garden that May was most beautiful.

The next day a few of their friends had been invited to dinner and amongst them were Mrs Ruttledge and her son. I had always been an admirer of her husband, Hugh Ruttledge, who had been the leader of the British 1933 expedition to Everest by the northern route, and also of the 1936 expedition by the same route. On the latter I had been one of the younger Sherpas in the party and that was the true beginning of my mountaineering career. I had been selected by Eric Shipton and W. J. Kydd from a whole bunch of candidates, although I had none of the right chits and no certificate of previous experience with an expedition.

It was hard work on that early expedition. Sometimes we carried as much as ninety pounds on our backs, but higher up, of course, much less, only fifty-five. Up and down, up and down we went, until all the food and equipment was in the right place. So much was new to me then: equipment I had never seen before, and material like ropes and axes I had seen but never handled. And all the various kinds of mountain work were an unknown experience. I began to learn them on the Ruttledge expedition all those years ago. At that time I was not yet twenty-two, yet I carried to North Col at over 22,000 feet despite my inexperience. For I had been born to work at heights and my heart and lungs were made for them. Besides, I had had this dream about Everest.

For this reason the Ruttledge expedition has a special place in my memory and I was particularly happy to meet Mrs Ruttledge so long afterwards. It was hard to believe that a great war had taken place in the interval, that politics had changed the face of the Himalayan world entirely, that Everest had been climbed not once only but many times, not from the north but from the south, that Tibet was now a closed land, and that I myself was nearly sixty years of age.

Yet I well remembered how, during that 1936 expedition, after returning with Frank Smythe and Eric Shipton and Captain Halsworth from a path-finding climb on the steep north face, Mr Ruttledge had said to me in perfect Hindi: 'Look now! Everest will not go anywhere. It is there and some day a man will climb it. Don't be in a hurry. I don't want you to kill yourselves by being reckless. You will always have another chance to try climbing this mountain if you are not successful this time. ' And so it turned out. When Everest was climbed at last there was not a single casualty on Lord Hunt's expedition. Men have died there since.

We spent two wonderful days with the Jenkins and then they drove us to Wales, to the Pen-y-Gwryd Hotel. There we met all the surviving members of the 1953 expedition, except for Hillary, with their wives and children and grandchildren. Lord Runt's daughter was there with an infant of two months. So also were Eric Shipton, Professor Odell, whose connection with Everest was the longest of all, and Sir Christopher Summerhayes, who had been the British Ambassador in Nepal in 1953, and others who had been connected with or had helped the expedition. My nephew Gombu, who has climbed Everest twice, was there too, with his wife Sita.

The weather was kind to us and the reunion lasted for a long weekend. We were thirty-eight in all and after a press conference on the Saturday the whole party walked up the Miners' Track to Glyder for a grand picnic. The party divided for rock-climbing on the Glyders and Bristly Ridge and for a traverse of Tryfan. Lord Hunt and Mrs Westmacott took Daku on to Bristly Ridge for her first rock-climb ever, up Great Tower Buttress. It was most successful; Sally Westmacott said of Daku afterwards that she is a natural rock-climber and that on this climb—graded a 'severe'—she simply 'floated up'. She certainly enjoyed herself. I was not with them. I did no climbing at all. I kept Gombu's wife Sita company— she does not climb—and we walked among the mountains and enjoyed the grand views of the Welsh mountains and valleys. And I helped by taking the climbers' sacks back to the hotel.

On the next day we went over Craig-yr-lsfa, a fine mountain of precipitous crags, and there Daku climbed again, this time with Michael Westmacott on what is called Amphitheatre Buttress. This she enjoyed as on the day before. Meanwhile I continued the long walk up the ridge that ends in Carned Llewelyn, a great plateau with a cairn to mark the highest point and a fine view that on the right day stretches to the sea.

Back in London on 29 May we went with Lord and Lady Hunt to the Royal Geographical Society's meeting to celebrate our anniversary; the film was shown again and Lord Hunt gave a speech after dinner. It was a moving occasion. We stayed for a while with the Hunts at their home and this was when Daku, who had for a long time wanted to learn to swim, had her first lessons in the Hunts' pool with the great mountaineer as her teacher.

We remained in England for several weeks after that. We visited many friends. It was especially good to find June Kirkwood again; she was living in Haslemere in Surrey and we stayed with her there for some weeks, during which she took us on a short trip to Scotland, where I saw the wonderful Highland cattle for the first time—not unlike yaks, it seemed to me. During this period, too, I spent a good deal of time with Malcolm Barnes discussing this book and recording parts of it. He, too, lived in Haslemere and was a friend of Dr Feuz of Zurich, through whom we had come together. I recall that the flowers that summer were wonderful and the scent of the roses in Malcolm's garden was so strong in the warm morning air you became aware of it before you even reached the house. Then in July we left again for Zurich with Malcolm, to talk with Ernst Feuz and to join a party of Swiss comrades that was organised for me at Interlaken—and finally home. We had been away for two months and there was much to do. And again, we missed our children.

15: A TIGER GROWING OLD

In this book I have not been able to tell you, as I did in my first, the story of a great climb and of its long preparation. What you have been told instead is the story of the building up of a great school of mountaineering in a land where climbing was still a young sport of which most people knew nothing at all, and of the progress of a middle-aged tiger through a world he had never expected to see, among people he had never expected to meet, into a hopefully comfortable retirement.

For not an idea of any of these developments was in my head in the times before the 1953 expedition, nor even as we fought our way through the Khumbu Icefall and the Western Cwm to South Col and the final summit. Only when we were down and back to the towns and the crowds did I have the suspicion that nothing would ever be the same again. And it was not. I suppose I thought, if l thought about it at all in the days before the great climb, that the rest of my life after the expedition, whether successful or not, would go on much as it did before, with jobs coming my way from time to time with this expedition or that and long spells at home if I was lucky. Nor had I any idea that the effects of a success on the people of Nepal, and the Sherpas especially, would be so deep. As I have said, later on some thought of this began to dawn on me, especially when politics and personal jealousies began to show up.

Certainly nothing that I—or the whole expedition—could then do would have made any difference; the changes would probably have come anyway, even had we and later expeditions failed or succeeded. Like others, I have had my own ideas about how we could even now modify the effects of change, but I cannot know whether they would work or whether it is already too late.

Looking back over my sixty-two years I suppose it would be quite true to say that the ascent of Everest was the high point of my career in two senses of the word 'high'. Up to my fortieth year this had been my ambition and my dream. Then the dream was fulfilled and for a little while I must have been the most satisfied man on earth. Yet in reaching the summit I had not only achieved my ambition; I had also been freed from it. I did not have to think about it again. In fact, I had no desire at all to go to the top again—not like Gombu—and this was not from lack of interest or disappointment; it was simply that the thing had now been done, the dream fulfilled, the purpose of all that hard work and planning made clear— at least to me. Now I could think of other things, do other things, go other places.

I recall that I once asked a Swiss mountain guide how many times a year he went to the top of the Matterhorn, and he answered 'only' twenty-five. But this was his job. This was business and not a personal matter, not a question of pleasure either. It was commercial. In my own part of the world I go up and down the same Sikkim slopes many times a year without reflection, and that is my job; it is not pleasure, though there is real pleasure to be gained from turning out a really good climber from among my students. Everest is something different; it could never be a job, at least for me. It never was, right from the beginning. I did what I set out to do, and to repeat the climb would not give me much satisfaction.

Even after twenty-three years Everest is still very close to me. It is a beautiful mountain, but it is not necessarily a dangerous mountain—unless you go out to find danger and you can do that on any mountain anywhere. There are, moreover, difficult and dangerous new routes besides the one we took all those years ago. But I do respect this mountain; there is something fascinating about it apart from the fact that it is the highest in the world, and there is something very natural about it. I was never quite sure that we would get to the summit, although I knew that someone would do so one day, and in a way it was a bit of luck that I happened to be one of the victorious pair, Hillary and myself. It could well have been another pair. I did not go in order to be famous or rich; I did it because I wanted to. And if the chance had not fallen my way, who knows what might have happened afterwards?

Up there it was very simple. One succeeded or one failed. One lived or died, to put the question to the extreme alternative. This is what I mean by 'simple'; the choice was clear and it was one's own. It was when we came down again that the difficulties and complications began, such as I had certainly not foreseen. And they proved more exhausting by a long way than all the climbing, and my health suffered in consequence. Once off the mountain, if there is no injury or frostbite, you recover in a short while from the exertion, but it takes you a long time to recover from the strains that other men can put you to. Anyway I was ill afterwards for quite a while. The problems that faced me then took a long time to work off and to this day I am very cautious to avoid all entanglement with political schemings or arguments, or with any personal jealousies, which in fact are very common in mountaineering relations.

Besides having no real desire to repeat the Everest climb, even for sentimental reasons, my work has prevented me from taking part in expeditions or private climbing of my own, but at the same time, as I have shown, it has kept me very close to the mountains and to mountain people, and I reckon that I spend more time and energy each year climbing up and down in Sikkim than do most members of famous expeditions and their men, who are only occupied for short periods and a few seasons. For twenty-three years I have been climbing for months each year and journeys abroad have been the real breaks.

Looking back now I do not think that Everest, though a great achievement, gave me the most memorable moment of my life, or even the best climb.

Sometimes a failure can provide something more memorable, like my experience with Raymond Lambert in the Spring of 1952. That was really exciting, much more exciting even than the successful climb the next year. So was the second Swiss expedition in the autumn of the same year. This is because we were then climbing where nobody had ever climbed before and facing problems no one had had to solve before. We were breaking entirely new ground. In the spring expedition everything ahead of us was unknown, completely unknown, and this is why it left such a deep impression on my mind. Once we started to climb the great Khumbu icefall none of us had any idea what we might find in the hours or days ahead. Up till then only Tilman in 1950 and Shipton in 1951 had taken a close look at the icefall. Their view was that the fall was extremely dangerous and probably impossible to pass, especially for a whole expedition. But we did get through and that is something I look back upon with special pride, for once we had proved we could pass the fall others could pass too, and so they did during the years that followed. The same, of course, can be said of the final climb to the summit a year later with Hillary, for nobody knew what was up there in the last thousand feet beyond where Lambert and I had been stopped.

Anyway, the unknown world did not stop with the crossing of the icefall. We were the first to set foot in the Western Cwm, the first ever, and that was exciting too, as well as what we saw of the way ahead. We were the first to cross the Cwm, the first to reach the South Col, and the first to venture on the ridge that was eventually used in reaching the top a year later. So it is not difficult to understand why I still think of the 1952 spring expedition as so specially memorable. Everything was so new, so unknown. We were real pioneers.

Another reason for satisfaction was that, because we did not know what to expect and what special equipment we might need, we had to invent as we went along. We had not brought along with us any of the ladders and portable bridges that expeditions use nowadays. We did not know we needed them until we had actual experience of the icefall, and then we had to make our own from wood brought up from the nearest forests. A lot of what we made vanished as quickly as the ice moved, crevasses opened or closed, or great blocks of ice crashed down and swept everything away. The great icefall was moving continuously, never the same from one day to another, or even from one hour to the other, groaning, creaking and exploding as it forced its way down, visibly moving and breaking up. Today climbers can get through it in a day; in those days we had often to camp in the midst of it and I remember that huge crevasses could open in the night right beside your tent and cut you off from what you had thought was an easy route. We used more than a hundred bridges on that first attempt and we had to make them all—ten-foot, fifteen-foot bridges, and even longer. And all the wood had to come up from Thyangboche and its neighbouring forests.

Yet it was not the ice that beat us in the end, for we won the struggle for the icefall; nor was it exhaustion, nor fear of the unknown; it was simply the Everest wind. The same thing happened in the autumn of the same year. Of course it was exceedingly cold, but we were protected against that by proper clothing. Against the wind we simply could not move or stand. And it never seemed to stop. Even when we left the mountain for good the wind could be heard roaring away across the ridges.

To the mountains I am especially grateful for the friends they gave me, friends all over the world and in all sorts of occupations—soldiers, lawyers, doctors, teachers, farmers, writers, engineers, photographers, all united in the same love of high places no matter how different they were in other ways, and I have remained in touch with almost all of them, though some have died during the years since we were in the mountains together. To name only a few of those whom I particularly remember might appear like selecting the famous and forgetting the rest, but that is not true; from many mountain-loving people whose names are not well-known at all I have received very great kindness and help, and I have felt for them a closeness that only comes from a deep love of the same activities. There are too many such people to name them all here.

I think especially of all the members of the Swiss and British teams on Everest during 1952 and 1953 and the problems and dangers and the pleasures we shared. Many of them I still meet from time to time at reunions and celebrations and then it is as if the years between had never been more than weeks. And many of them write to me or come to Darjeeling or I have gone to see them in their homes in, Switzerland or England. How happy are our meetings!

Pandit Nehru, to whom I owe so much for help and friendship, has been dead now for many years; he was like a father to me and when I had troubles I took them to him and he was generous with advice, very kind and understanding, and very wise. It was he who helped to extricate me from the political troubles that surrounded me in 1953, and it was he who encouraged strongly the founding of the Institute and my appointment as Director of Field Training that has been my main activity ever since. I hope that I have justified his faith in me: I have not created a thousand Tenzings, as he had asked, but I believe I have done something to create in India a mountaineering tradition that is growing fast and strong.

Lord Hunt was a wonderful leader and he got the complete loyalty of us all, and he too from time to time has given me much-needed advice, which I have always tried to follow and remember. Especially important to me was the advice he gave me when we were on our way back from the great climb and he warned me against the people who would use me for their own purposes if they could. Working under him on Everest was an experience that no one could ever forget. On that expedition we had no great arguments or disagreements, whereas on other expeditions I have known or heard about there has been a lot, especially when they were finished and the climbers got home. What is more, no single climber on John Runt's expedition made money out of it; all the earnings from books (except my own, which was made a special case) and films and lectures and articles went into the central fund which has since then done so much to support and encourage other ventures and journeys of exploration. For me Lord Hunt is a great and good man, and over all the years he has been most friendly to me and helpful, as well as a warm and welcoming host whenever I have been in England.

In this book I have mentioned Raymond Lambert many times. For him I have a quite special affection. A big, happy, humorous man, and a great mountaineer, with whom I almost got to the top of Everest a year earlier than its actual conquest, and with whom I shared all the exhaustion and disappointment of that failure, if that is what it can be called. To Raymond's home in Geneva I have been many times; so have my wife and elder daughters. As I have said already, it is almost a second home to me. I never visit Switzerland but I find myself on the way to visit him, and that is often; we exchange frequent letters to tell each other what we are doing, and I had the great delight of receiving him in my own home town of Darjeeling at the 1973 meet.

I had not met Raymond until the Swiss came to Everest in 1952, but we quickly became the closest of friends and have remained that way ever since. At that time he had already acquired a great reputation in Europe as a professional climber, and after his return from Everest he continued in that profession. The fact that he lost his toes from frostbite well before the war did not lessen his great skill and strength as a climber. He and his party had been trapped by a blizzard while climbing in the range of Mont Blanc and for several days were forced to take refuge in a crevasse; this is how the frost got him. The result is that he wears climbing boots that are curiously foreshortened and leave prints in the snow that are not at all like normal footprints ; in fact I once heard someone remark in fun that they probably gave people the idea that a yeti had been around in the night—that perhaps Lambert was in fact the abominable snowman.

Dittert introduced Lambert to me as a 'bear' (*balu*) and that is the name by which another great climber is affectionately known—H. A. (Bill) Tilman, whom I always regard as my Himalayan 'guru', since from him I learned a great deal of mountaineering, probably more from him than from anyone else. After the war, when he came back to the Himalaya, I was with him for three months in the Lang Dak range, not very high mountains, but we were not there for climbing; it was really a journey of exploration, for much of that country was then unknown. On occasions we were up above the snowline and crossing mountain passes; on others we were in deep jungle interesting ourselves in the vegetation and the flowers as well as the rocks. It was an exciting time, for me very different from the usual climbing expedition, and in those three months I got to know Tilman well, and it was a disappointment that I did not go along with him and

Charles Houston when, in 1950, they led the first party to the Everest region from the south and really paved the way to eventual success.

Then there is Sir Edmund Hillary, with whom I shared the great moment at the top of the world and who has done so much since then for the Sherpa people of Solu Khumbu, returning to the valley time and again to see them and to follow the progress of the hospitals and schools he founded. The trip on which he took Daku and me in New Zealand in1971 was a wonderful experience, and not the least pleasurable part of it was to see Sir Edmund in his own country amongst his own people.

With Frank Smythe I had a particularly close relationship, probably because I climbed with him to very high places so early in my career, when I was scarcely more than twenty years old and hoping for so much. I remember how I last saw him when he came out to Darjeeling in 1949 with the intention of climbing in Sikkim and I was to go with him. Permission for this small expedition had been obtained and all the Sherpas and porters and equipment were ready and waiting when permission was suddenly withdrawn. We never knew why. It was for Smythe a great disappointment; for me too. But within a few days he was acting very strangely and talking strangely as well. He did not seem to know where he was or what he was doing; he could not remember his own name nor the date when it came to signing his name in a friend's guest book. It was then that I knew he was very ill. Soon he was taken into hospital, but he did not know me, and later returned to England. Not long afterwards we heard that he had died, this very great and sensitive mountaineer, with a great love for the Himalaya and its flowers, who was one of the true pioneers of Everest, climbing so high on the northern routes. I have often thought about his death and wondered what would have happened had we been able after all to start on what would have been a last journey into the mountains; would the disease which killed him have struck him just the same in the middle of his expedition, far away from all help? Would we have got him back in time? Or would he have died up there in the mountains he loved? Perhaps he would have wanted it that way.

Professor Tucci was one who played a very big part in my life, mainly on account of the eleven-month journey I made with him into and through Tibet in 1948 in search of Buddhist art treasures, but one manuscript in particular, which he eventually found and was given. Apart from which he also bought or acquired a huge number of other Tibetan art treasures—thankas, sculptures, paintings, writings—all kinds of lovely things which amounted in the end to a great caravan of three hundred mule-loads when we came back through the passes. They went with him to Italy and I have seen some of them there. Tucci was a very strange, explosive, difficult, remarkable man. Many people—most people—could not work with him; Sherpas, porters he engaged on the journey, could not work with him and would leave him after a few days. But he and I managed to live with one another quite well and he trusted me entirely, even to the extent of looking after many of his transactions with the Tibetans and also his money, of which he carried a great deal on the journey. He had a disturbing habit of talking loudly to himself as he walked along, in all sorts of languages, bits of Italian, English, Tibetan, Hindi and so on, singly or all mixed up. I got used even to that!

It was on that journey that I first met the Dalai Lama. In fact I met him twice in Lhasa, and on each occasion he blessed us. At that time the Dalai Lama was only fifteen years old, but the Professor knew him well and was allowed to have quite long talks with him while I stood by and listened, which was an unusual privilege since in those days it was not thought proper to look at His Holiness directly.

Since then I have met him again on several occasions, once at Kalimpong when he first visited India on a pilgrimage tour, also at Darjeeling and Gangtok on the same tour. Then, following the Chinese disaster at Lhasa and the Dalai Lama's exile in India, I met him again in 1962 at Siliguri. Finally, in 1975, when His Holiness visited Darjeeling my whole family was fortunate to receive his blessing. I regard the Dalai Lama as a truly holy man; whenever we meet he always takes the opportunity to talk to me about mountaineering and once he jokingly suggested that I might take him up into the mountains.

When he visited Darjeeling in 1975 the people of the town turned up in thousands to greet him; never in the past had Darjeeling seen such a gathering and such enthusiasm. People of every faith and religion stood at the roadside eagerly awaiting his arrival. My family and myself have great reasons to be grateful to the Dalai Lama and his affection for us.

In 1948 we were in Lhasa for about a month, and during the ensuing months we tramped up and down the length and breadth of Tibet, visiting every conceivable monastery in search of the treasure that Tucci had long made up his mind he must have. It was a wonderful journey through what to me was the holy land and from the professor I gained an extraordinary mass of information; he could explain to me almost anything we set eyes on during our travels. Eleven months with such a man, very learned and deeply interested, is something to be grateful for and remember, even though he was so difficult to live with. All the more so because no one can do such a journey now and no one knows when it will ever again be possible, certainly not in our lifetime. A peasant might join a caravan crossing, as they still do, into Tibet from Khumbu, but not a professor from Europe and certainly not me. A few lovely things I brought back for myself and they are now in my home -not to mention the dogs I brought back which became the parents of generations of dogs that went on from Darjeeling to so many parts of the world. But the best thing I brought back from Tibet is my memory of that fabulous land, its monasteries and temples, the mountains, the city of Lhasa and its boots and equipment, and compare them with what I had on during the 1953 ascent, I am amazed and humbled. He must have been very strong to have achieved all that. At the end he was quite close to the point where Lambert and I gave up in 1952—just over the ridge in fact, scarcely more than a stone's throw away. So, although I never saw him, I find him very real. And it was he who stood one day on the pass to the north of Khumbu and decided that the key to the ascent of Everest might well lie in the southern approach, the route that led to eventual success.

And my fellow Sherpas of the fifties? Not many of them have much—if anything—to do with the mountains now. Some have died. Some have gone into business. Some have settled down as farmers. Some are in Darjeeling like me, but for a long time have given up mountaineering. All of us are growing old. As with the European climbers, time has taken its toll.

Now I am faced with yet another turning-point in my life: retirement. By the time this book is published it will have taken place, for I have been wanting to retire from my directorship of field training at the Institute for some time, but not exactly in the way it has happened. In fact, I was due for retirement in 1972, and I made clear that I wanted to do so, not because I could not carry out the job perfectly well for a long time yet. I am still as fit as ever I was in wind and limb and eye, and I can still turn out a fine number of accomplished students. But when I raised the point first it was because I felt that it was the right thing to do: the Institute was then twenty years old, well-established, with a succession of excellent instructors to choose from. It was time I handed over to a younger man. But then they answered, stay on for another year, another two years. So I said to myself, very well, one more year, two more years, carry on. So I carried on.

When the Institute was founded in 1954 in Darjeeling in preference to the claims that were put forward on behalf of other places, like Uttar Pradesh and Maharashtra, mainly because of its fine position, its suitability, its nearness to the Sherpa homeland, but also because it was my own home town, both Dr Roy and Pandit Nehru had verbally assured me that the job I was given would be mine for life if l wanted it that way. But they are both now dead and what they said all those years ago only I know. Of course, I should have got their assurance in writing. But I am a simple man; I have to trust people. And I looked to them to look after me. But the fact is, nevertheless, that the conditions I have worked under, especially in recent years, have not been comparable with those even of my own instructors. And so, although I would like to retire, I really cannot afford to do so. Except that now I must.

For instance, unlike the instructors, I have never had free housing in all those twenty-two years. It is true that I have a house of my own, but they should have given me a housing allowance instead. It is due to me as a government servant; yet I never asked for it, nor was it offered me. Moreover, my pay today is the same as when we started! Even though the price of a chicken has in the same time gone up from two to eleven rupees, to give only one example of our rising cost of living. This is something that should have been understood, and someone should have done something about it. But they did nothing. Nor have I, like the instructors, a pension to look forward to. Of course, I should have asked—for increases in pay, for pension, for allowances. I have done so for my men. But not for myself. I am not a beggar.

I gave my word to Pandit Nehru and Dr Roy and I have kept it. They assured me that the job was mine for life and that if I should want to retire the salary was mine for life anyway. They were my friends. One trusts one's friends. Now they are dead and things are very different. So after carrying on from year to year after once or twice raising the question of retirement myself—carrying on at *their* request—I am now told that according to Government rules I must retire, that I should already have retired. I do not blame the Government; I respect rules and regulations. But what happens to the promises I was given? So from May 1976, instead of being Director of Field Training I am to be an adviser.

Things do not look very nice for me and I am dissatisfied. If I had fore-seen from the beginning what I now know, I doubt if I would have joined the Institute at all, but have gone in for other things. The opportunities were open for me in many directions, but even if I had stayed in mountaineering I could have taken part in many expeditions, and I missed many chances that offered. Whereas, although there have been no less than three Indian expeditions to Everest in recent times, I was never invited to take part in them, just as I was never invited to take part in the celebrations after success was achieved, although I had trained some of the climbers! In fact, however much the rest of the world has accepted me for what I am, in India I have always been out of the show. And I do not really know why. I have kept the promise I made to Nehru, as the world can judge by what HMI has become, and I have at least the satisfaction of knowing that I have done my duty, not only to the Institute itself but also to Sherpas as a whole. For what distinguishes HMI from the many other mountaineering institutes that have sprung up in many parts of northern India is that it is the only one where all the instructors are Sherpas. This is what Panditji and Dr Roy wanted. This is how it is today after twenty-two years and I only hope that HMI will keep the tradition.

This brings me to another of the questions that has worried me over the years. Many people back in my homeland are dissatisfied with me, the people of Solu Khumbu and even the King of Nepal himself, because, they say, I left Nepal to live and work in India and have done nothing for my own people. Which is simply not true. Every year for twenty-two years the Institute of which I have been Director of Field Training has accepted young Sherpas for training as first-class professional mountaineers and I have helped to make them so. All our instructors have been Sherpas without exception. Some we have sent to

Switzerland for extra training. Sherpas are to be found in mountaineering schools and institutes in other parts of India who have been trained by us and have found jobs elsewhere. This is what Panditji wanted; he was determined that the Sherpas should get this special treatment, and our friends, the Swiss Foundation, were equally keen to see improvement in the status of Sherpa mountaineers. This we have carried out. And with this increased professionalism of Sherpa climbers has come an increase in their fame, which has benefited the Solu Khumbu both directly and indirectly, more so, I think, than if I had stayed in Khumbu—to do what? or even Kathmandu.

At least I have done much to bring fame to my valley, by the ascent of Everest alone, by all the journeys I have made to so many different parts of the world and the talks I have given everywhere. Wherever I have travelled – in Europe, Australia, New Zealand, America and Russia, also Japan—I have spoken as a Sherpa, even when I have been talking of HMI and India. I have spoken as a Sherpa when I have talked of Everest and its conquest, and of Solu Khumbu and its people. And in my first book I did the same thing. I have not done anything of this as propaganda. I am not in the diplomatic corps. I am not in the pay of any government, Nepalese or Indian, when I do this. Everywhere I have told the story of Everest and HMI because I think it is a good story, because I have believed in what I have been doing and want people to know about it. I do not think that the people of Nepal, on the one hand, or the Government of India on the other, have quite realised what in all these talks and appearances I have done for both their peoples over the years.

And so before the summer comes in 1976 I shall retire, but I have not decided what next to do. I do not suppose I shall have much difficulty in earning a living. I could always help with expeditions; I could take part in them. I can still go on climbing for a few more years, until I am seventy but not more. And in Nepal, if I go back there, I would not be out of a job. Having kept the promise I made to Panditji, but depending on how much I shall be occupied in Darjeeling as 'adviser', I could well go back to Solu Khumbu and work in some way that would be useful to the valley.

For instance I would like above all to open a climbing school there, not one with a big building and organisation, but one with a minimum of formalities, perhaps with a few huts in the neighbourhood of Lukla, where the air-strip now is. Just big enough to house the students, not more than twenty at the start, and perhaps a few tourists too. It would be only thirty-five minutes by air from Kathmandu and four days' march from Everest base camp. A lot of climbing can be done from there and it would be a great help to the young Sherpas and eventually to the whole Solu Khumbu.

I think a lot of people all over the world would want to help in setting up such a school. The properly trained young men would no longer go off to Kathmandu to find work as guides or porters, or leading trekking parties, waiting and waiting for maybe two months for a job to turn up and then one month's work. The money is soon finished and at home there is a neglected farm. With a good mountaineering school and Sherpa climbing centre in Solu Khumbu these men would be able to live on their farms with their families and look after the cattle and the crops and have climbing work close at hand, just as in alpine countries. It would be a much better way of living, and the money would stay in the valley too, and not be spent in thecity.

For such a school we would in time need staff. When we started in Darjeeling we had only a very few people; today there are sixty employees. The same thing could happen in Solu Khumbu. All this would make employment and stop the drift away from the valley. It would help to bring the farms back into cultivation again, so many having fallen into disuse because the people have gone away or there are no men to work them. To my mind it is a bad thing that the farming people and farming tradition should go, for it was what held the Sherpas together. Without the farms the population may well disappear and Solu Khumbu become empty.

So far the expensive hotel at Shyangboche has not really helped a lot: the workers to build it were brought in from outside, it was staffed by Japanese, and the food they serve comes either from Kathmandu or India. Perhaps there is work there for a few Sherpa women washing dishes, but what real good is that?

Recently an offer was made to buy up the whole area around Khumjung, including the village itself, so as to build another air-strip there. This would have destroyed the farm lands there too. Sir Edmund Hillary, who has a hospital and a school there, would not agree to such a plan. I was asked my opinion too, and I said no: maybe the Japanese will give you a lot of money, but you should not think of one generation only, you must think for ten generations ahead, and this money is not enough for ten generations, not even a million rupees.

It is not only the men who go away, though they go first. The young married women go too. What else can they do? The men who wait for work in Kathmandu and sometimes join expeditions or treks cannot easily return to Solu Khumbu and may never return. The distance is too great and they do not earn enough to allow them to fly backwards and forwards. To be left alone in the valley for months is no life for a girl. So away they go too. Houses that stay empty for so long soon fall into ruin and that is exactly what has happened.

The story of Daku's own family is typical. Daku herself came to Darjeeling for a holiday and stayed to marry me and have her family there. Two of her brothers followed her and we gave them a good education. After that I said to them, you are educated now, you should go back to Khumbu and not neglect the farm any more. But they said no, they would not go back. I could not make them do so. There was little I could do, though I did turn one into an instructor at the Institute, while the other took employment in the Indo-Tibet Border Police. It is the same with one of Daku's sisters. For a few years now she has been with her husband in Kathmandu; sometimes they say they will go back to the farm, sometimes they say they will not. I do not think they will ever return; they have been away too long. For them Solu Khumbu is finished.

Two winters ago I was in Khumbu and I went to see Daku's family home. There is only one brother left there in the mountains with the farm and the yaks, and the parents are now very old. The old people are always crying, always asking how things are, when the children will be coming home. They say they are too old now to do much about the farm, so the one brother looks after them and everything else. The end cannot be far off.

It is like this with so many up there. The yak herds are getting smaller because there are not the boys to look after them as I did fifty years ago, and the potato fields on the slopes are going back to weeds. Such a pity! Such a beautiful country!

This is where my plan for a climbing school comes in. One day the valley could be even more popular with tourists and climbers than it is today and I believe there will then be a real need for properly trained Sherpa climbing men on the spot. Why should they and everything else be brought in from Kathmandu or even farther afield? Although Everest has now been climbed by many parties, men will still come year after year to climb the world's highest mountain, just as they queue up to climb the Matterhorn in summer and as many people in fine weather trample about on top of Mont Blanc. These expeditions will need trained men, men with greater experience than guiding groups of tourists along mountain trails, although that too could be catered for, since not everyone coming to Khumbu would want to do real climbing. And it is not a matter of Everest alone; all around are many great mountains for the climber and lovely valleys for the walker. The need for trained Sherpas could bring real prosperity to Khumbu.

This is not happening yet. But perhaps one day they will build a road up the valley and then build hotels too and other tourist facilities as in Switzerland long ago. Then the Sherpas will stay, to guide the tourists and climbers, work in the hotels, even own them, till the fields and provide the food. This may take years, but I think it will come. Meanwhile, a Khumbu climbing centre and school would be a start. And I would once more be able to live in my own land and do something for my own people.

Lukla would be a wonderful place for such a centre. From there you would take your time walking up the valley, plenty of time to acclimatise and enjoy the surroundings. It is a very beautiful world and there is no need to hurry. There is no need to go to the Everest base camp at all, as nearly everyone does today, and I suppose for a long time people will want to do so. It is not by any means the most beautiful place in the region; there is finer scenery elsewhere: the side valleys, all very lovely, with marvellous climbing if that is what you want to do, and splendid trekking and camping country, and a whole world of grand mountains to look at, such as you will never see anywhere else in the world in such numbers and splendour. You could stay for weeks up there if you have the time to spare, and in March and April the weather is just perfect.

I seem now, in looking back, to have lived three very different lives, each of them satisfying, each of them happy, each of them rewarding in its own way: the life of a boy in the high pastures with the yaks, which ended with my departure for Darjeeling; the life of an ambitious young Sherpa mountaineer based on Darjeeling, which ended with the conquest of Everest; the life of a teacher of other climbers, that kept me away from other mountain adventures but sent me to far distant lands I never dreamed would be within my reach, to meet people of many kinds and occupations and interests. I am a lucky man, I have always admitted, and I am a happy one.

To write a book like this is a matter of looking backwards at the past, but, as I said in *Tiger of the Snows*, in living one must look ahead. I have said something of the plans that have passed through my mind in thinking of the future. Whether they will bear fruit I cannot tell. But I had one great dream when I was young— to climb Everest—and that came true. Why not another?

Then there is my still young family. For years yet I can watch them grow in body and mind and this is my greatest pleasure today, and in the years to come I can watch them make their ways in the world and know, perhaps, that my determination to see that they all received the best possible education has borne fruit. Whether any one of them will take to the mountains I do not yet know. I doubt it. They are all too young yet to have formed any ideas about their futures, and when their education is finished they will make their own decisions. One or the other may turn to the mountains purely for pleasure, but as a source of income— as a job? I think not. We shall see.

Meanwhile I repeat the words I said at the summit of Everest as I covered up the little offerings I had brought along—the cat, the pencil and the sweets -'Thuji chey, Chomolungma'. I am grateful, Chomolungma....

A PORTRAIT OF TENZING NORGAY

I had not met Tenzing at all until he came along to me one recent summer and talked about the book he wanted to write -or rather, wanted me to write for him - about his life since the descent from the first successful climb to the summit of Everest. I had set eyes on him only once before, and then from a distance soon after the event. I remembered his earlier book (the one written for him by James Ramsay Ullman, *Tiger of the Snows*); I remembered, too, the newspaper photographs and stories in 1953, the man on the television screen, and most of all the excitement the whole story created when it reached London on Coronation Day 1953 and took us all by surprise. I recalled especially the incredible smile on the face of the Sherpa in all the newspapers when the photographs came through of his triumphant progress through India (which caused no little trouble), the fine features, the quick clear eyes, and the splendid teeth. And here he was, talking to a tape-recorder about the past, and about his plans and ideas, a man of nearly sixty years in 1973, but looking much younger than that, strong and spare and self-possessed, and still apparently a very active mountaineer.

Even as he talked I realised that the great days of 1953, when with Hillary he conquered the world's highest mountain after so many attempts, were indeed a long time past. And at the back of my mind was the question, inevitably: does anyone care now about Everest as we cared then other than Tenzing's own generation everywhere, who shared the excitement, and that international body of mountaineers to whom the event will not fail to be significant always as the summit achievement of the golden age of world climbing?

Myself when a boy had read all the literature on Everest that was then available, and through the years before the war had followed the efforts of succeeding expeditions. To me—and to many of my generation—Everest meant adventure even before I set eyes upon a European mountain, and the men who went out to climb it were to my youthful vision somewhat bigger than human. Mallory and Irvine were to me as heroic as were Captain Scott and Captain Cook and a score or more of other such explorers. But now that it has been conquered, can Everest possibly mean anything like as much to those who have been born since? As you will see, Tenzing asks the same question; yet the story still finds audiences of all ages, as Tenzing finds on his world-wide travels.

It is difficult, however, for those who did not share it to realise the intense excitement of those days. Hitherto unknown outside his own community and the centre of Himalayan mountaineering, Darjeeling, a simple Sherpa, a man of no formal education, Tenzing got to the top of Everest and came down an incomparable hero to at least half the world, for the people of Asia especially. He became, so to speak, an instant legend; to millions, literally, he became a demigod. '*Tenzing zindabad*—'long live Tenzing'—was the shout that greeted him from thousands of throats in the villages he passed through on his way back, and in Kathmandu, where the crowds took over and roared their delight, as they did later in the great cities of India. To all these Tenzing began to symbolise Asia, Asia triumphant.

Medals were showered upon him—then and through the years that followed: first the George Medal from Britain, almost at once, and the Star of Nepal from King Tribhuvana, and others from India, France, Italy, Russia, America, from national institutions as well as local ones, and from learned societies (the Cullum Medal of the Royal Geographical Society and the Hubbard Medal of the American National Geographical Society among them), and many more in the years of travel. Places were named after him: in Hemel Hempstead, in Hertfordshire, there is a Tenzing Road, and there is another in Southall, Middlesex, and there are probably several more in other parts of England, in company with Hunt, Hillary, Wylie and Gregory roads.

Receptions were given for Tenzing everywhere he went, and opportunities came to talk to private clubs, to school groups and university societies, during twenty years and more, even to the present day, close on a generation after his triumph. Nehru became his friend, patron and adviser; and indeed he needed one, as people tried to latch on to him for 'political' purposes and involve him in national rivalries.

Was he a citizen of Nepal? Was he a citizen of India? Each nation tried to grab him for itself and the press, especially the Eastern press, clamoured for an answer. Tenzing's own answer was as clever as it was simple: he was born in the womb of Nepal and raised in the lap of India! Who got to the top first, the Sherpa or the New Zealander? Another loaded question, seeking to set the members of the team against one another and produce national antagonisms. To the mountaineers the question was of little or no importance: they were a team and they succeeded as a team. To the 'politicians', to much of the press, the answer seemed to be of enormous importance. People tried to trap Tenzing into saying things that were by inference a denigration of his British colleagues. Fortunately he had already been put on his guard against a situation that was outside his experience, and his strong natural intelligence helped him to avoid the worst troubles.

Yet the 'troubles' left their mark and even to this day the fear of 'politics' brings a sign of anxiety into his otherwise happy expression. It passes over his face like a cloud. At the thought of saying something that might offend, that might be construed as taking sides in some remote Himalayan quarrel or political incident, his mouth tightens, the forehead furrows deepen, the eyes take on the look of a hunted creature as he reaches out to switch off the recorder and explain his position confidentially. In the weeks immediately after the climb the pressures were very real; people lost their tempers, wrote or said things they afterwards regretted. Newspapers printed reports that had little substance behind them or were wholly untrue. And all because a Sherpa sirdar to a British expedition had realised a dream that had obsessed him since boyhood, of one day standing on the summit of Everest, which he had seen so often from the pastures where he tended his father's yaks.

The mistakes and misunderstandings of 1953 were not all on the Asiatic side. Even in Britain people were heard to recall—quite unnecessarily—Tenzing's menial occupations during his earlier Darjeeling years and to describe him as 'a cocky little man'. Actually he is far from little: of average height and proportionately broad, and I have never noticed anything particularly arrogant about Tenzing today. Happy and self-assured certainly. Proud of his achievement he has a right to be; so would any of us be in the circumstances. Nothing more. Yet Tenzing can be most proud of a quite different achievement: the success of the Himalayan Mountaineering Institute in Darjeeling, of which he has been Director of Field Training since its inception twenty-two years ago. Ex-pupils of this school, apart from its instructors, have succeeded brilliantly in many difficult exploits in the Himalaya. In 1965 eight Indians and one Nepalese from one expedition got to the top of Everest, of whom seven had been associated with the Institute or had been trained there. Gombu, Tenzing's own nephew and deputy, is the only man in the world to have reached the top twice.

The importance of that first ascent in 1953 is evidenced by the frequency with which the story is retold and the fact that audiences could still be found for it many years later, as far away as New Zealand and California. It really captured the public's imagination as told by the Sherpa climber. Since 1953 many men of many nations have gone to the summit and some have followed much more difficult routes, though it must be remembered that the first British expedition to succeed had broken through a vital psychological barrier, and that in twenty years the equipment available to climbers has been developed enormously. Yet the story of the first ascent, after so many failures, will, like the story of the struggle for the South Pole, never be forgotten and will be repeated through many generations even when the mountain itself, like the Matterhorn long before, has become a relatively commonplace climb.

And Tenzing at sixty? The brilliant smile, the wonderfully expressive and mobile features, are still there; a leaner, harder face perhaps, and certainly more lined, but full of intelligence. For make no mistake: Tenzing Norgay is a very intelligent man, a fact that strikes one on very short acquaintance. He is also a loyal and generous man, careful not to give offence to anyone, appreciative of kindness and honesty, expecting them quite naturally from others and surprised when such expectation fails, as it does from time to time. A proud man, too, speaking only rarely of his grievances and of his own inability to put them right, but saying in conclusion, 'I am not a beggar', as though that settled the matter.

Writing an autobiography for another man has obvious difficulties, especially when that man is of another race, with a vastly different background, who speaks English volubly but with difficulty, owing to a severely limited vocabulary. He uses even familiar words, simple and everyday words to us, with different meanings every time, through lack of an alternative, but the changes in his voice make the change of meaning clear. The problem is made worse by the fact that Tenzing neither reads nor writes in any language whatever, giving his story straight from memory. He has no written records for the writer to examine and exploit, no diaries, no letters written with his own pen, no note of any kind of any event as it happened. Yet his memory is phenomenal, possibly because it has had to compensate for the lack of documentation on which the sophisticated and the literate habitually rely. When it comes to names—of people or of places—Tenzing gives them as he heard them and remembers them, but voiced with his own Sherpa style of speaking and stress-ing. To him the name Pen-y-Gwryd, where he attended Everest celebrations, a difficult enough name even for an Englishman, is not a matter of nine letters visualised as spoken, but a sound which he has heard others make and repeats as best he can. He cannot check it for himself and he cannot help another by spelling it out or writing it down. When it comes to using Himalayan placenames the problem is even worse and only by constantly running and re-running the recorded version does the truth emerge, with the help, of course, of maps and other books. It is a slow business. Similarly, to one born of a Tibetan tribe in a then remote valley, a tribe whose chronological system is perhaps picturesque but not particularly exact, dates are not of the same significance as to a Westerner. Where important events are few one day is much like another and does not require a special label. When it is a question of what month the answer is easier even than the year; it can be fixed by the season and the weather, at least approximately, but not always what year. Sometimes when you question Tenzing about a date you sense an irritation; he is not sure and you feel him asking whether it matters anyway. And he could be right.

Yet we need dates to get a story's proper sequence estab-lished. And such dates as I have obtained needed careful verification. Some dates could only be fixed as a surveyor fixes points on a map, by their relation to other known points, and it is possible that some are still not right. Tenzing could not until recent years establish the date of his own birth, beyond the fact that he was born in the year of the Hare, which comes round every twelve years, so that he could have been born in 1902, 1914 or 1926. Clearly it must have been 1914. But beyond the year he can only state that it must have been late in May, because of what he has heard about the state of the crops at the time. He got to the top of Everest on 29 May and he thinks that 29 May is a very good day for his birthday too.

Now that we are involved in explanations something should be said about proper names and family relationships among the Sherpas. Family names—or surnames—do not exist as we know them. A child is named a few days after birth, but he does not take on a father's name with it. And it can be changed later without difficulty and without formality, as was the case with Tenzing himself. When he marries, the wife does not become Mrs Tenzing, nor does a daughter become Miss Tenzing. Tenzing's wife remains Dawa Phuti, as she was before, or Ang Lahmu, as she too was before her marriage; the girls remain Pem-Pem and Nima, as they were named when born, and Tenzing is not part of that name. Tenzing admits to a clan name: Ghang-La, but he uses it only as the name of his Darjeeling home; it is actually the name of a tract of land given to an ancestor in return for warrior services rendered to a ruler. Ghang-La was part of Tenzing's father's name, but it did not come down to Tenzing himself. Tenzing has been known by other names: Tenzing Bhotia is one, and Tenzing Khansama, both clearly of a descriptive nature. Today, for official convenience, he has added Sherpa to his name, though it is not, strictly speaking, a part of it.

As concerns family relationships, it should be remembered that Sherpas are of Tibetan origin and until recently had followed Tibetan customs and traditions more or less. In Tibet polyandry and polygyny were customary until quite recently, and amongst Sherpas too. When a woman married a man, she married his brother or brothers too. No emotional or jealousy problems resulted. Sherpa men did not find any difficulties about the sexual side of a polyandrous marriage; nor did Sherpa women find any difficulty about being one of two wives of the same man. The custom of polyandry certainly served to keep property within a family and saved it from being progressively fragmented; and, of course, Sherpa women were rarely alone—when one husband was away on a long journey, the other or others were still there. But although these customs have virtually died out in recent times—for economic reasons and as a result of contact with the Western world—there is no law against a man or woman having more than one spouse. Polyandry was always more common than polygyny, and the most frequent motive for a man taking a second wife in the lifetime of the first was childlessness. As a Swiss mountaineer observed to me in a letter, 'the solutions found by other races and peoples to overcome familiar problems do not lag behind our own in social and human relationships but rather outstrip them'. However, one product of these multiple marriages of the past is the complexity of the relationships between one person and another; you can build up quite a lot of relatives of varying degrees of closeness in a generation or two. Hence the terms cousin or sister are not necessarily as exact in their meaning as they are with us.

A Sherpa village home is by our standards a cramped affair, at any rate until recent times it was and probably still is in most cases; all the members of a family live and sleep in the same room. This is the traditional lifestyle and does not infer a state of squalor or great impoverishment; far from it. But in this one-room life the activity of any individual does not seem to have been particularly restrained by the constant proximity of others; for instance, the daughters of the family pursue their amorous adventures by night in the presence of their parents and other members of the family. Such circumstances make for the tolerance and good humour, spontaneity and lack of prudery that characterises the Sherpas and for which they are renowned. They are indeed a happy people, as anyone who has travelled with them will know, tolerant and good-humoured to a high degree, finding enjoyment in almost anything they do, interested in everything and with a strong sense of fun, a word chosen deliberately in preference to humour. Tenzing himself is typical, as his famous smile betrays. His delight in living is deep and infectious and vigorous; his interest in all things human and natural (as opposed to technical things like speedboats and skyscrapers) is deep; his laughter genuine and contagious. Even in his puzzlement at some of the people and situations he encounters there is an element of laughter; after a pause the deep wrinkles vanish from his forehead and the smile returns as he says in conclusion, Funny!' In his usage the word is nevertheless ambiguous: it means firstly that he probably does not like the person or thing concerned, but also that he finds in it a mirth-provoking element.

But how long the Sherpas' simplicity and happiness will survive against the inflow of Western ideas, habits and standards, is open to question, a matter about which Tenzing, as this book shows, worries greatly. They have lost much of their tradition already and their language almost entirely. What we regard as Sherpa character is not necessarily in-heritable; tolerance, good nature, a sense of fun, spontaneous friendliness—these are not passed on with the blood, so to speak, but are the product of tradition, environment, physical conditions, isolation. And when these factors change, the Sherpas will change, as indeed they are changing already. In places like Toong Soong Busti, where they live in Dar-jeeling, they have preserved their characteristics because they still live as a relatively compact community. But those who have migrated to parts where there are no other Sherpas or few of them, are rapidly absorbed into the population, adopting the ways and outlook of those around them.

Much of this story was tape-recorded first of all. It was then gradually enlarged through endless questions and correspondence and research; letters sometimes took a long time to reach Tenzing because he was frequently away from Darjeeling with his students in the mountains of Sikkim when they arrived. Then an intermediary came into action, who had to read my questions to Tenzing and then transmit his spoken replies. This introduced another hazardous element, where perhaps the intermediary could not interpret exactly or my questions were badly phrased. Then further questions had to be asked. Thus what began as a skeleton, more or less, slowly took on flesh, but I think most of the problems were solved. Many people—British, American, Swiss and others—have given great help in filling in the details, and this is acknowledged elsewhere.

It is probably unnecessary to add that a spoken story is a very different thing from a written one. It would be quite impossible to print exactly what Tenzing said. It has to be translated, so to speak, into relatively conventional written form, with due regard to grammar and syntax, but I hope that some of the simplicity of the original thinking has survived and some of the spontaneity of the man. In any case I had often to suggest the right words while the recording proceeded and to offer clarifications for approval.

Tenzing's use of some words is very expressive, as I have already hinted, in spite of his small vocabulary. For instance, the word 'terrible' is a favourite one, but it is used with a great variety of inflection and emphasis in combination with intense facial expression and body gesture. All this is impossible to register in a written tale. You just have to hear it. When Tenzing says of the wind on the crest of Everest at 28,000 feet in an icy dawn that it was 'terrible', this is no flat statement: you can feel, through the sound he makes mouthing the word, the enormous pressure of the gale, the deathly cold, the clouds of flying snow, the brutal buffeting of body and mind, the tearing and shrieking and the demonic din, the weariness and the fear and indecision that makes a man deny his ambition, turn around and retreat. Yet Tenzing will use just the same word to describe some social bore from whom he had sought vainly to escape, and –again as spoken—it has taken on a quite differ-ent meaning, half-malicious, half-amused, and you can see the meaning in his look.

Gesture is important too; a haughty lift of the jaw, with half-closed eyes looking along his nose, fingers pulling at his chin, or the twisting of his lips—all these and others convey as much of Tenzing's opinions as do his words. And the expression of his eyes changes constantly, as they light up or cloud or seek pene-tratingly for information from what is going on around him. Twenty-one years ago Ullman spoke of being somewhat enamoured of this man called Tenzing' and adds that even if he had never heard of Everest he would still have recog-nised 'the rare and wonderful quality of the man'. These words were written under the immediate influence of the climb and its aftermath, but they are quite valid today. No one could meet this Sherpa mountaineer without succumbing in some degree to the strength of his personality, and without sharing in his spontaneous enthusiasms, quick sense of fun and genuine warmth of feeling. He can be exceedingly enter-taining in small company. About his uncomplicated mind and directness of approach to any problem there is something slightly disconcerting, because he does not at once assume difficulties as the rest of us do. When he makes up his mind to do something, he goes and does it; and if you suggest it cannot be done, he looks puzzled but is not put off. It is impossible not to think that there was something of this in his approach to the idea of climbing Everest, as if he weresaying,'So we are going to climb Everest. OK, let's go!' This is, in fact, the attitude which has taken him around the world, through lands where he does not know a word of the lan-guage, and cannot read it anyway; if he needs to travel from A to B he just sets off, does not listen to impossibilities, but gets there.

True, Sherpas as a whole are an outstanding people, but Tenzing is outstanding among them or in any company.

As for his physique, it is equally phenomenal. Remember that this man is now past sixty, and yet for years he has been climbing up and down the mountains of the Himalayan Mountaineering Institute's training area in Sikkim to the height of 21,000 feet and more—not once only, but many times a year, watching his students at work, group after group, week after week. Like, he observed to me once, a Bombay taxi driver. No wonder he can assure one that he could climb Everest again today, though he does not want to, because it would give him little satisfaction. He gets as much mountaineering in the course of his teaching as any man could want and a great deal more than most accomplished mountaineers ever do in their whole careers. And he has been doing this for twenty years.

His purpose in having this book written and published is two-fold. First, like any honest maker of books he wants and needs to make a little money. His second family is still young and he is determined that they shall have the best possible education, and would like them to end up with some education abroad, hopefully in America. All this is expensive. Secondly, he has strong feelings about the fate of his native valley, Solu Khumbu, where the social changes of the past two decades have been radical and not wholly beneficial. The things he deplores and what he would like to do to put them right he explains in various parts of his book, but primarily he wants to stop the depopulation of Solu Khumbu consequent upon the trend of emigration to Kathmandu and elsewhere; he wants to revive the farming which has degenerated because there are no longer the men to do it, even if they wanted to; he wants to revive the original Tibetan language and culture in some degree, to stop the pollution which has resulted from increased tourism, and to create sources of employment which will bring the people back to their ancestral lands and homes.

Tenzing's relations with his native Nepal are not entirely good. It is said there that he has deserted them to work entirely in India and they, the Nepalese, are not pleased. But he explains that while he has worked for the Institute he could do nothing else; he had given his word to Nehru that he would work for the Institute as long as he was needed. When he retires he will be free to do other things, and these he explains in some detail. Anyway, that he has done nothing for Nepal and the Sherpas is far from true. He has given the Sherpas a world-wide image; he has regularly trained an annual intake of Sherpas at the Institute; he has helped to establish proper levels of pay and status for Sherpas on expeditions; he has helped to lay down rules to protect Sherpa climbers' interests.

Speaking in November 1957 at the centenary dinner of the Alpine Club in London, at which Tenzing was the Club's guest, Sir John Hunt (as Lord Hunt then was) said:

'Not only did Tenzing share with us what some will hold as being the biggest of all our adventures, and take part in a great many other adventures with members of this club and other British climbers, but his people have helped ours for more than a century to explore and enjoy their wonderful mountains …. (Tenzing's) integrity is such that, despite four and a half years of world adulation, he remains a simple, modest and warmhearted man. '

To this praise Lord Hailsham added:

'Tenzing is one of the group of very famous men who are referred to quite simply without prefix or suffix…. Tenzing has won fame all over the world, not only for what he has done but for the qualities of spirit and character which have made him known and loved and respected wherever he has been…. What an ambassador he has been for a people who for many centuries lived secluded in their mountains and valleys and are now for the first time to be fully known and admired by the majority of mankind. '

This is a just estimate of what Tenzing has done for his own people, quite apart from the work done on their behalf in Darjeeling.

Otherwise this book is a simple narrative of twenty years of work, of adventuring and travelling all over the world, of raising a family in the shadow—in more senses than one—of the Himalaya. I wonder how many people of my own generation must have paused at some time over the years and asked 'Whatever happened to Tenzing?' This is the answer. Quite a lot happened to Tenzing and not all of it what you might have expected at the beginning of this second phase of his life.

Until the descent from Everest in 1953 the author had never travelled far from the Himalaya. Sudden fame took him to distant lands he had never seriously thought about, introduced him to the famous and the powerful, showed him other mountain ranges and other ways of life, exposed him to curious forms of exploitation, but always he came home to the world he understood and lived again in the shadow of his own mountains. He knows when he is being made use of, but is never impolite. If he finds he is to speak to an audience not of the kind he expected or for an unexpected purpose, he keeps his word and does not complain. He loves people everywhere; he is not interested in machinery or nonhuman things; he loves his family and works for them ceaselessly; he is deeply interested in animal life and is absorbed by his dogs. The experience of wide travel and of fame have not spoiled him.

In a book of this nature the spelling of placenames and proper names is a problem. Fortunately the more important names are already standardised, but still the valley that leads to Everest is spelt in four different ways (Solu, Solo, Sole and Sola Khumbu), while the variations in the westernised spellings of Sikkimese and Bhutanese placenames seem equally numerous (Pemayongtse, Pemayongchi, Pemiongchi, etc.). One can only try to be consistent.

Malcolm Barnes, 1977

Printed in the USA
CPSIA information can be obtained
at www.ICGtesting.com
JSHW021939120424
61082JS00004B/7

9 781783 342518